The Rapid Vis Toolkit

Presenting new and unique drawing tools to help you to rapidly and effectively visualize your ideas

The Rapid Vis Toolkit

An Intriguing Collection of
Powerful Drawing Tools
for the Rapid Visualization
of Ideas

Kurt Hanks

Crisp Publications
Menlo Park, California

Credits

*The following people have been important
in the development of this book:*

Editor: George Young, Crisp Learning
Copy Editor: Sal Glynn
Contributor: Jennie Hanks
Contributor: Michael Lee, Michael Lee Design
Contributor: Prof. Fendell P. Furtenur
Cover Design: Fifth Street Design, Berkeley, CA
Printed in Canada By Printcrafters Inc.

02 03 04 05   10 9 8 7 6 5 4 3 2 1

Library of Congress Card Catalog Number: 2002108144
Hanks, Kurt
Rapid Vis Toolkit
1-56052-675-0

Contents

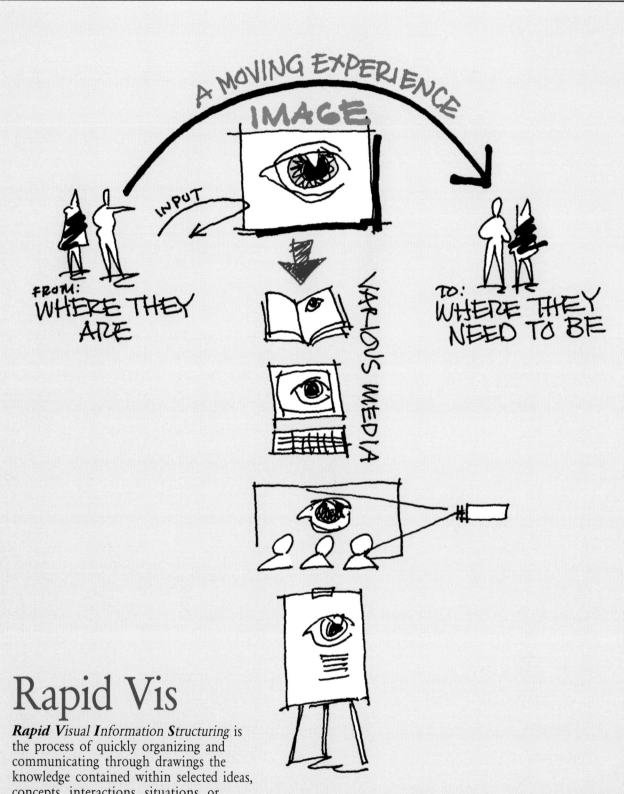

Rapid Vis

Rapid Visual Information Structuring is the process of quickly organizing and communicating through drawings the knowledge contained within selected ideas, concepts, interactions, situations, or contexts with the purpose of creating some meaningful change.

Rapid Vis for Rapid Change

This is not your typical drawing book. The subject matter in this book is about a kind of drawing, but it's not the kind of drawing they teach you in art school. It's not that things like perspective, color, and layout, aren't important, it's just those subjects aren't what this book is about.

On this book's pages drawing is presented as a tool for thinking, learning, and communicating. Drawing is treated here as a tool for the visualization of ideas, concepts, and possibilities in a rapidly changing world. Drawing is expanded into a much wider role than what is usually thought of, facilitating change being at the center of that new role. Let me illustrate with a few stories.

The first story happened when I was teaching a college design drawing class. After the first assignment, a student pinned her drawing to the wall. Poor kid, her drawing was so overworked that you could see light shining through the drawing if you held it up to the window. It had been erased and reworked far too many times, more like something hand sewn than drawn. I asked the student how many hours that she had spent on the drawing.

She hesitantly replied in a tired voice, "Oh, I think about 60 hours." I believed her.

Another story is about my interaction with another professional designer. We were both working on a project and had a lull in all the activity. We began chatting. Laid out on his desk was a beautiful drawing that he had recently completed. Every line was perfect and everything in the drawing was just right. It was more a piece of artwork than an evolving design.

I asked this designer how long it took him to complete this drawing. Without hesitation he said, "Two and a half weeks." That immediately took me back. I had to steady myself from falling over. I've never had that kind of time. My drawings and sketches are always due yesterday. Most of the other designers I know echo the same words. There is never enough time to ever spend two and a half weeks on any drawing. →

All the drawings in this book took only a few hours at the very most to finish and many of them took only a few minutes.

1
Introduction

Here is another story. I had to attend a combination conference call and meeting but I was late (traffic problems). When I finally got there everything and everybody was going nowhere. This was an important meeting. Decisions had to be made then and there. Much depended on this meeting's results and none were forthcoming. Still, knowing this, I also fell into going the same direction everybody else was headed and went nowhere with them.

That is, until I started to draw on a large white board. Drawings pull information and ideas together into a unifying focus better than anything else. As the lines, shapes, and notes started to appear, everyone in the room collectively focused on my developing drawing. Suddenly the entire direction of everyone, including those we faxed an image to over the phone, shifted

into what needed to be done. They stopped struggling with each other and jointly moved that struggle into the drawing. Like so many times before, a drawing made a nomadic meeting stop wandering around and actually accomplish its intended purpose.

One last story: it's about a drawing someone else made. A foreign student was taking an American history class. The student had to take the class, but it was irrelevant to their life. But this was a different kind of class. The students drew images and extracted principles in this class.

I can still see this student's excitement at learning a principle and making an interesting little drawing of how the principle she had just learned in American history applied to her own personal life. She had no

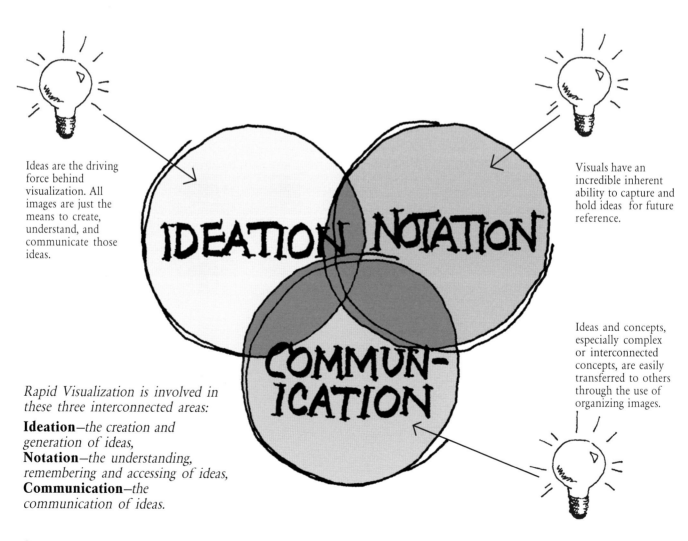

Ideas are the driving force behind visualization. All images are just the means to create, understand, and communicate those ideas.

Visuals have an incredible inherent ability to capture and hold ideas for future reference.

Ideas and concepts, especially complex or interconnected concepts, are easily transferred to others through the use of organizing images.

Rapid Visualization is involved in these three interconnected areas:
Ideation—*the creation and generation of ideas,*
Notation—*the understanding, remembering and accessing of ideas,*
Communication—*the communication of ideas.*

art background, but the drawing communicated well. It was a little drawing that served as a link between a formerly irrelevant subject and the deep problems this student was having with her family back in Japan.

This and similar stories actually make two points. First, drawings take too long. Things are moving faster and faster and we don't have the time to wait while we carefully polish our drawings. What is needed are faster ways to get those images on paper, faster ways to get ideas across, and quicker ways to use drawings to get the results we need and want.

When used in a slightly different way drawing can be effectively used to a great advantage in areas and in ways not usually thought of as being in its domain. This kind of drawing (or the name I would rather call it—*rapid visualization*) packages information into knowledge. And that is what we need much more of. We are drowning in information, but we are sorely lacking in knowledge.

Knowledge is structured information, and images can powerfully provide that structure. Images allow information to be made useful, understandable, and all the important things at the center of what I feel is the meaning of real knowledge. →

When transformed into the rapid visualization of images, drawing has a much wider variety of effective applications than usually thought of.

In many of these areas drawing is as powerful a tool as in its usual art and design applications.

And there is one more advantage. Visualization in these areas is a relatively new application. There is an excitement and wonder whenever the process of rapidly creating images is used.

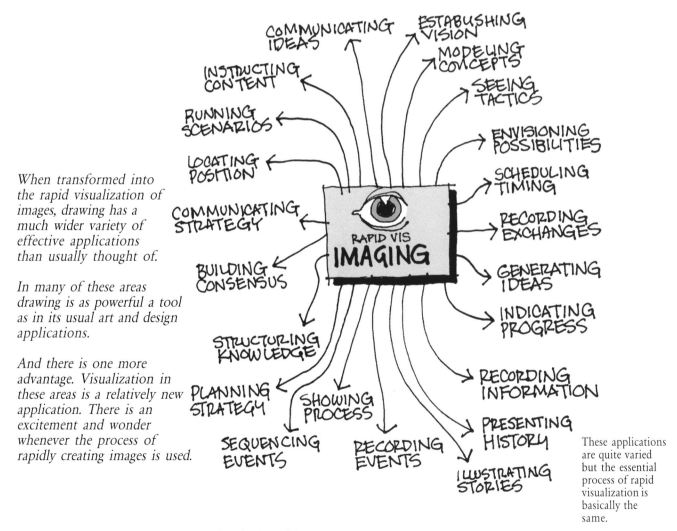

These applications are quite varied but the essential process of rapid visualization is basically the same.

NOTE: With the expansion in these areas of application of the *Rapid Vis* process also comes expansion of the impact on anyone using this process.

1
Introduction

Where typically drawing is an intuitive and aesthetic experience with the end result being an expressive image, Rapid Visualization uses drawing as a means to an end not an end in itself. Visualization has to do with the structuring of information for a desired response. All the over 400 drawings in this book were created to do the one thing of causing change, to bring information to bear on a choice that shifts thinking. *(That is why I use Rapid Vis, meaning Rapid Visual Information Structuring.)*

Information and its structure is not the usual fare of a drawing book. But it's the soul hidden behind every idea, image, and word of this book. The fact we live in

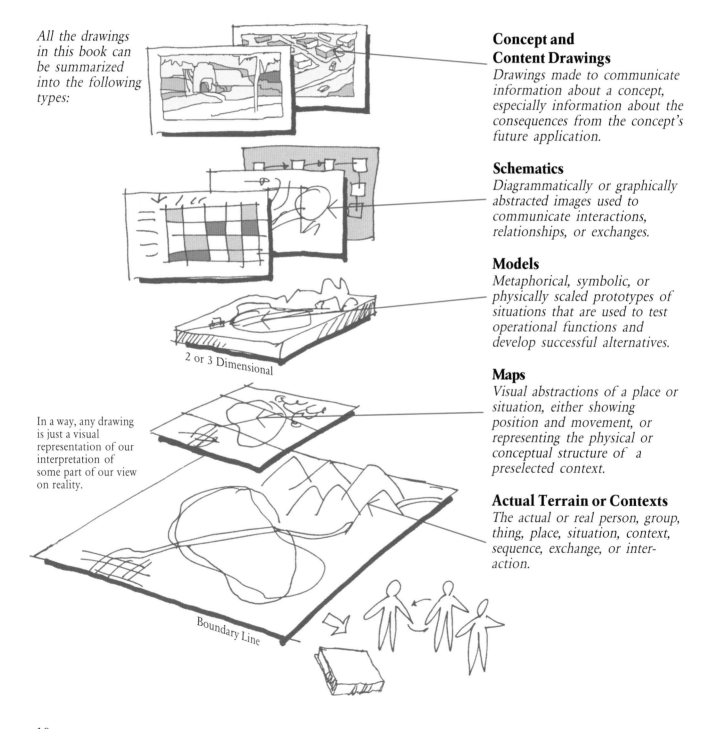

All the drawings in this book can be summarized into the following types:

2 or 3 Dimensional

In a way, any drawing is just a visual representation of our interpretation of some part of our view on reality.

Boundary Line

Concept and Content Drawings
Drawings made to communicate information about a concept, especially information about the consequences from the concept's future application.

Schematics
Diagrammatically or graphically abstracted images used to communicate interactions, relationships, or exchanges.

Models
Metaphorical, symbolic, or physically scaled prototypes of situations that are used to test operational functions and develop successful alternatives.

Maps
Visual abstractions of a place or situation, either showing position and movement, or representing the physical or conceptual structure of a preselected context.

Actual Terrain or Contexts
The actual or real person, group, thing, place, situation, context, sequence, exchange, or interaction.

the information age has been said too many times. But the fact that drawing is a powerful tool for this information age has rarely been said at all.

Designers and artists of all persuasions are an odd lot. They are often eccentric and driven. I've never met one who wasn't to some degree frustrated at not be-

ing able to have more impact with their craft. I'm no different. I've used Rapid Visualization in its expanded role for years for that very reason. This book is a compilation of all that time and experience. I hope you find it helpful.

*Rapidly visualized images fit along a **Scale of Refinement** ranging from spontaneous sketches, done on paper and taking only a few minutes, to full color rendering-like drawings, taking a few hours to finish.*

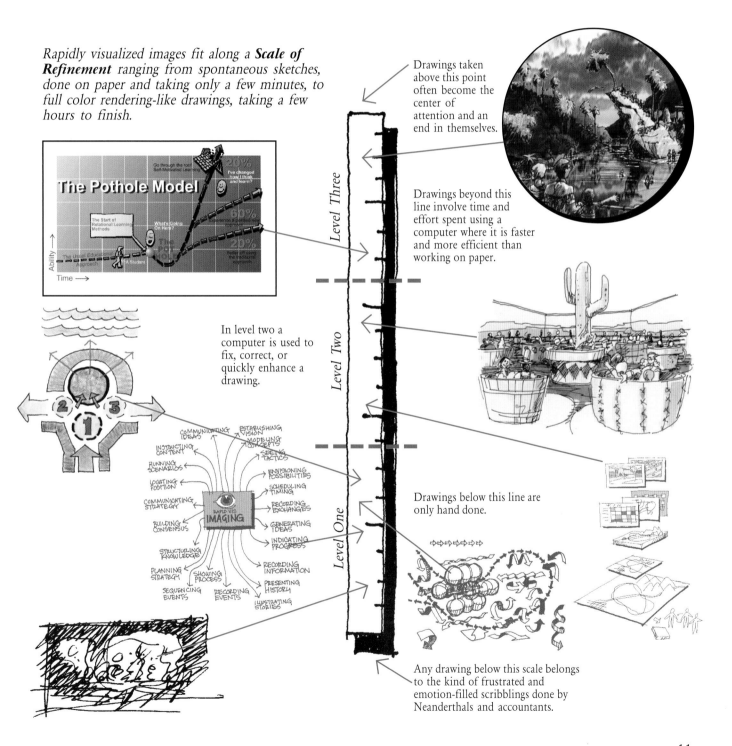

Drawings taken above this point often become the center of attention and an end in themselves.

Drawings beyond this line involve time and effort spent using a computer where it is faster and more efficient than working on paper.

In level two a computer is used to fix, correct, or quickly enhance a drawing.

Drawings below this line are only hand done.

Any drawing below this scale belongs to the kind of frustrated and emotion-filled scribblings done by Neanderthals and accountants.

2 Creative Standardization

Creatively Focus on What Counts

I used to have every design and drawing tool you could imagine. I thought it was a wise to invest and have any tool, paint, paper, or gizmo I could possibly ever use. I put it all in a large case with a handle and carried it around with me. I figured I always had whatever I needed when I needed it. I suppose being a Boy Scout taught me to always be prepared. Then I came to my senses and I gave it all away, including the stupid case. I've never seen more happy and dumbfounded designers in my life than the group I gave it all to.

The Standard Sheet *This sheet size (8 1/2 X 11) is standard for most business applications, such as filing, loose leafs, copy machines, and fax machines. Most of my Rapid Visualization drawings are also this size. Any change in this size has cost me both time and thought.*

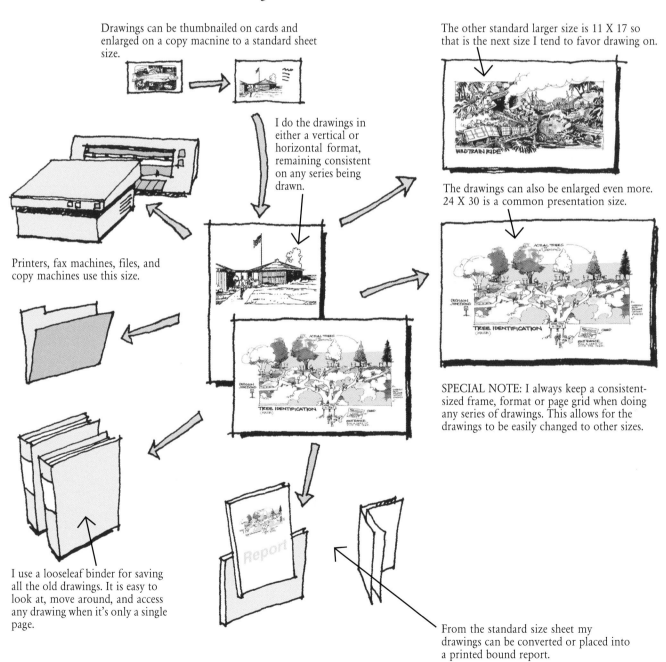

Drawings can be thumbnailed on cards and enlarged on a copy macnine to a standard sheet size.

The other standard larger size is 11 X 17 so that is the next size I tend to favor drawing on.

I do the drawings in either a vertical or horizontal format, remaining consistent on any series being drawn.

Printers, fax machines, files, and copy machines use this size.

The drawings can also be enlarged even more. 24 X 30 is a common presentation size.

SPECIAL NOTE: I always keep a consistent-sized frame, format or page grid when doing any series of drawings. This allows for the drawings to be easily changed to other sizes.

I use a looseleaf binder for saving all the old drawings. It is easy to look at, move around, and access any drawing when it's only a single page.

From the standard size sheet my drawings can be converted or placed into a printed bound report.

Every designer I've ever known that is really good at drawing has settled down to skillfully using only a few good tools. Anything else encumbers their creative efforts. I try to standardize every part of my drawing process because that isn't where my creativity is focused. I concentrate on where the innovation is needed, not on the drawing's size, my lettering, the drawing tools I use, or any other supportive materials. It's the old proven rule that your get 80% of your results from 20% of your actions. *Creatively focus on the 20% that counts; standardize the remaining 80% of what is left.*

The Hand Arc *This is another standard—the arc of my hand (approx. three feet). This arc is the basic unit I use to size any larger drawings done in front of a group. It makes drawing large much easier because it's a drawing module to replicate over the larger surfaces of white boards and flip charts.*

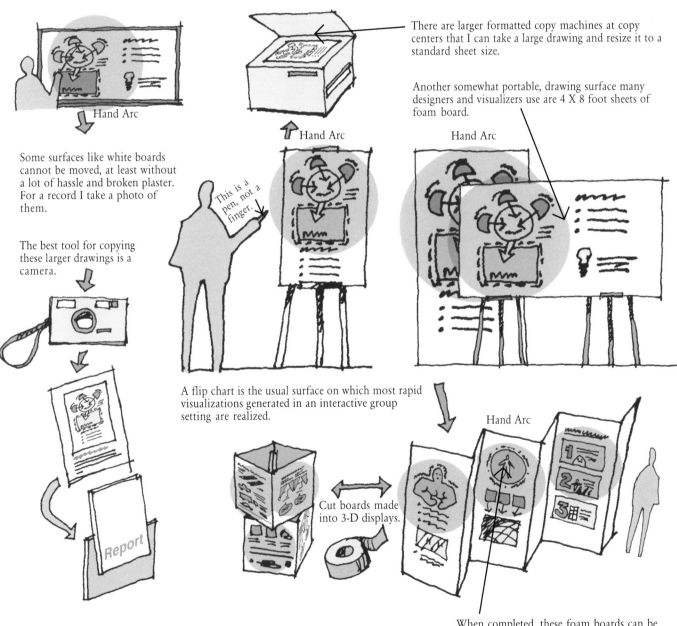

Hand Arc

Some surfaces like white boards cannot be moved, at least without a lot of hassle and broken plaster. For a record I take a photo of them.

The best tool for copying these larger drawings is a camera.

Report

There are larger formatted copy machines at copy centers that I can take a large drawing and resize it to a standard sheet size.

Another somewhat portable, drawing surface many designers and visualizers use are 4 X 8 foot sheets of foam board.

Hand Arc

Hand Arc

This is a pen, not a finger.

A flip chart is the usual surface on which most rapid visualizations generated in an interactive group setting are realized.

Cut boards made into 3-D displays.

Hand Arc

When completed, these foam boards can be made into an entire exhibit to present the ideas being recorded.

3 Power Tools

Making The Tools Disappear

My basic tools are uncomplicated and easy to obtain and use. Any technology I use is always in a supportive role. This is not because of some high sounding moral value about creative expression, but because I've been caught too many times with unstable programs and unattainable materials. If your value depends on your skill, and that skill depends on complex tools that fail, then nothing puts the impetus to simplicity like having too much failure with complexity. Over time, I have kept simplifying how and what I use.

Tools for Group Drawing *These are the drawings I do in front of a group. I collect and refine the ideas of everyone involved, including myself, and then rapidly draw those ideas onto a large visual representation.*

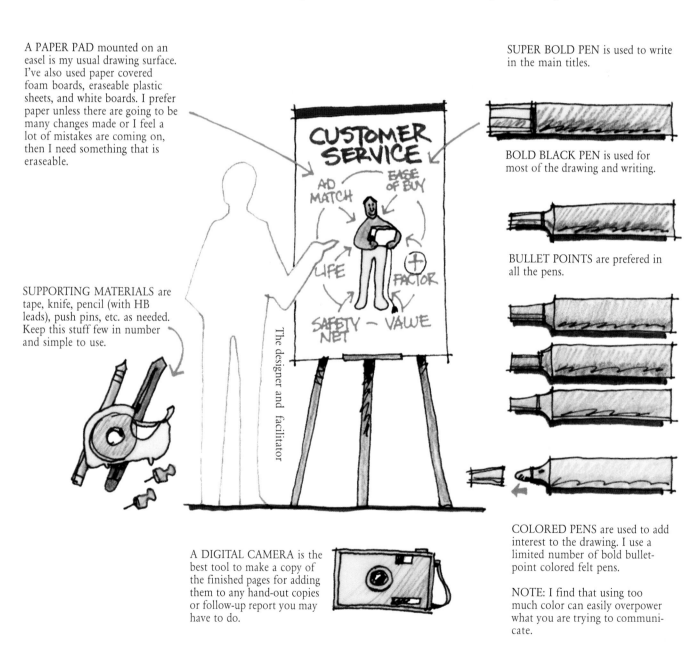

A PAPER PAD mounted on an easel is my usual drawing surface. I've also used paper covered foam boards, eraseable plastic sheets, and white boards. I prefer paper unless there are going to be many changes made or I feel a lot of mistakes are coming on, then I need something that is eraseable.

SUPPORTING MATERIALS are tape, knife, pencil (with HB leads), push pins, etc. as needed. Keep this stuff few in number and simple to use.

The designer and facilitator

SUPER BOLD PEN is used to write in the main titles.

BOLD BLACK PEN is used for most of the drawing and writing.

BULLET POINTS are prefered in all the pens.

COLORED PENS are used to add interest to the drawing. I use a limited number of bold bullet-point colored felt pens.

NOTE: I find that using too much color can easily overpower what you are trying to communicate.

A DIGITAL CAMERA is the best tool to make a copy of the finished pages for adding them to any hand-out copies or follow-up report you may have to do.

CUSTOMER SERVICE

AD MATCH · EASE OF BUY · LIFE · FACTOR · SAFETY — VALUE NET

When I simplified my tools something interesting happened. I became more skilled with less noticeable tools. Any great tool in the hands of someone who knows what they are doing will disappear. The tool becomes an extension of their hands to express their creative power. Whether in carpentry, music, or in the rapid visualization of ideas it's essentially the same process of using a few tools well. *"Keep the tools you use as simple as possible"* is the best advice I ever got. (The second best advice is, *"and don't tell clients how simple it really is."*)

Tools for Personal Drawing *These are the only tools I use when I'm drawing alone or when I'm drawing within design teams. Working with any more tools slows everything down.*

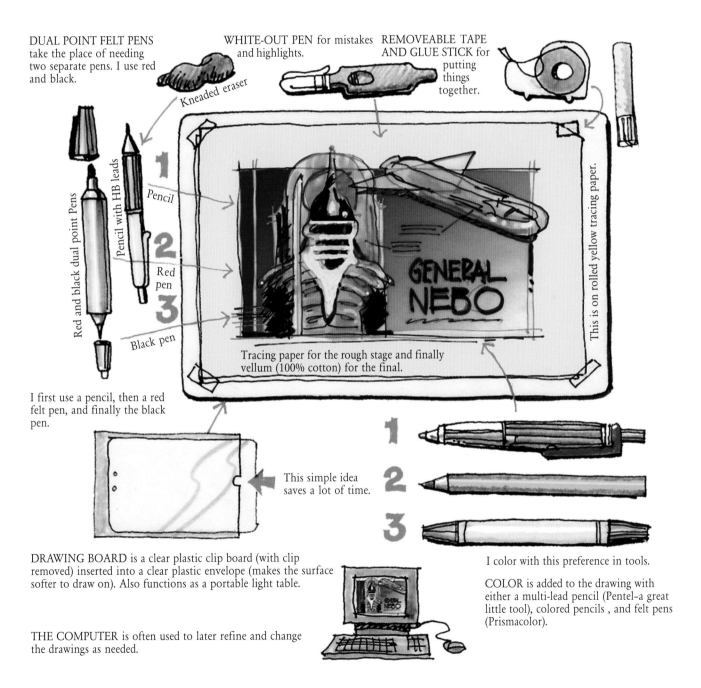

DUAL POINT FELT PENS take the place of needing two separate pens. I use red and black.

Kneaded eraser

WHITE-OUT PEN for mistakes and highlights.

REMOVEABLE TAPE AND GLUE STICK for putting things together.

Red and black dual point Pens

Pencil with HB leads

1 Pencil

2 Red pen

3 Black pen

This is on rolled yellow tracing paper.

GENERAL NEBO

Tracing paper for the rough stage and finally vellum (100% cotton) for the final.

I first use a pencil, then a red felt pen, and finally the black pen.

This simple idea saves a lot of time.

1

2

3

I color with this preference in tools.

DRAWING BOARD is a clear plastic clip board (with clip removed) inserted into a clear plastic envelope (makes the surface softer to draw on). Also functions as a portable light table.

COLOR is added to the drawing with either a multi-lead pencil (Pentel–a great little tool), colored pencils , and felt pens (Prismacolor).

THE COMPUTER is often used to later refine and change the drawings as needed.

Content Framing

Rapidly Visualizing Content

The major purpose of the drawings in this book is to communicate content. In the visual synopsis of a meeting, this content communicating purpose is obvious, but with more spatial or abstract drawing the purpose becomes more subtle.

The border of a drawing frames the content. A series of interrelated drawings frames a sequence of content with each frame building on the previous one. Even within a drawing are blocks of content building ideas, concepts, and knowledge.

↘*Here is a visualization of the total content from a talk showing how I reframed its content on to five pages.*

One part of this process is reading what is content, the other part is visualizing it.

↓*Often, the fastest way to do any final presentation drawing is to first do a totally content driven drawing with the key decision makers on what the presentation drawing is to accomplish.*

This is a very different way of seeing drawing and visualization. The usual approach centers more on communicating understanding than providing a method for personal expression. The viewpoint is born more from informational concepts and theory than the creation of art. It uses the wealth of knowledge contained in the art, but with a uniquely different attitude.

When the acts of conceptualizing and drawing are seen as primarily performing this function, a major shift in thinking happens in the mindset of the visualizer. Drawings then become more effective at what they were intented to do. Drawings are done faster, with less effort, and better achieve their purpose.

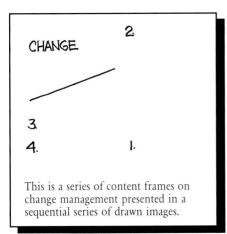

This is a series of content frames on change management presented in a sequential series of drawn images.

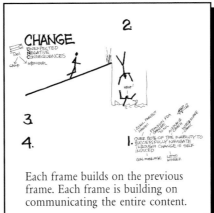

Each frame builds on the previous frame. Each frame is building on communicating the entire content.

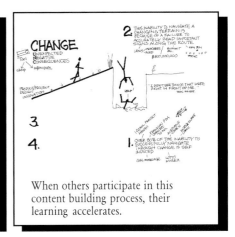

When others participate in this content building process, their learning accelerates.

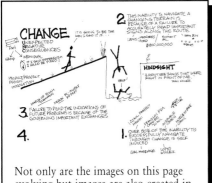

Not only are the images on this page evolving but images are also created in the stories being told.

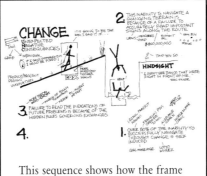

This sequence shows how the frame changes and grows into an overall communicating image.

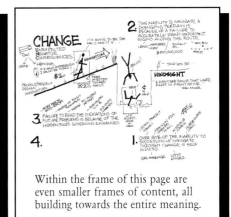

Within the frame of this page are even smaller frames of content, all building towards the entire meaning.

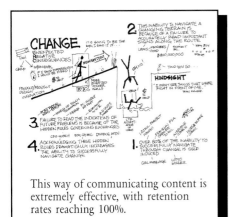

This way of communicating content is extremely effective, with retention rates reaching 100%.

As the frame nears completion, all the parts (or subframes) fit, achieving an overall cohesive meaning.

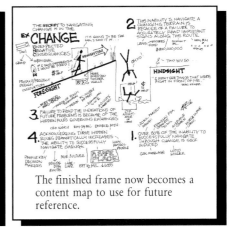

The finished frame now becomes a content map to use for future reference.

A Secret To More Effective Drawings

The strength in rapid visualization lies in making images quickly to achieve a desired response in a selected audience. The most important factor in to achieving this is creating an effective sequential flow of impressions and information within the viewer's perception.

The secret for an effective sequence is in making it conscious. That is, to deliberately and overtly lay out your drawings into a predetermined sequence. Most sketching is emotional and intuitive, but often you can deliberately plan, render, and place your images into logical and ordered steps or stages that will make your drawings much more powerful. Get a handle on the flow of perception and information in your drawing rather than leave it to chance.

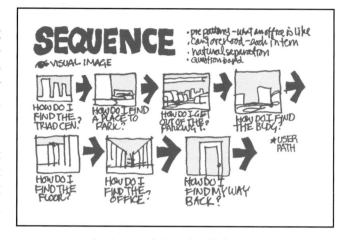

↑ *A set of thumbnail images for the route traveled to finally arrive at an office entrance. This drawing helped in roughly determining signing locations.*

↓ *This is a simplified and dimensionalized traffic flow plan for a museum. A flat flow diagram wasn't enough for the client to comprehend the concept.*

→ *Before and after images of a proposed golf and water park. Taking photos and then doing drawings of the proposed design is a very effective sequence.*

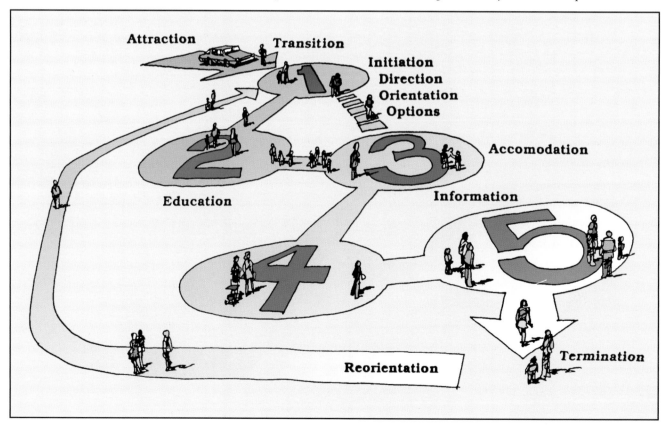

Existing View

Enlarged vew showing proposed future additions and landscaping

Pond   Waterfall   Center

Proposed View

Berm   Rest Area   Rough   Golf Course

↓ *A set of panels for a business meeting that were not pinned to the wall all at once, but one at a time, in order to encourage greater involvement.*

Some possible sequences you can consider when you plan your image's sequence.

Numerical 1-2-3 or Alphabetical A-B-C We have been taught since birth to follow a set order. Making these steps or stages obvious, like actually numbering or lettering your images, can establish a set order of viewing.

Chronological *Before-After, Beginning-End, Past-Present-Future. Visualized histories or biographies follow this kind of sequence.* Presenting images and only showing one at a time, building towards a completed chronology or map, works very well in many presentations.

Progressive *Simple to Complex, Easy to Hard, Familiar to Strange* When introducing information to the viewer you may want to choose this approach. Anything very complex and you may have no other choice.

Logical *Specific to General, General to Specific, Inductive or Deductive, Cause then Effect, Action then Reaction, Need then Benefit, Problem then Implication, Problem then Solution, Question and Answer* Logical order is already built into our minds and preset into our cultural attitudes. This makes for preestablished sequences that we can hang our images on for maximizing their impact.

Discovery *Put the Load On the Viewer, Here and There, This then That, Take it as it Comes* This way of sequencing allows the viewer to participate. If there is enough time for them to order your information-laden images, then this might work the best.→

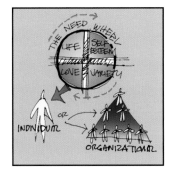

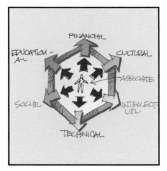

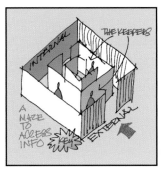

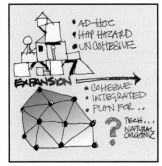

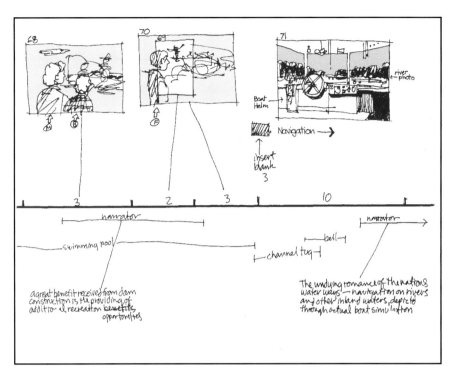

← *Thumbnail drawing sequenced in a storyboard format to determine the timing of a short film.*

→ The sequence of the viewer's eye was a conscious thought as I drew this image. The balloon at the top pulls the eye up and the ship at the end of the street stops the eye from going out into the river.

↘ A set of drawings for a restoration project that was started by first showing a dimensionalized floor plan. All other drawing views were developed and presented from that floor plan.

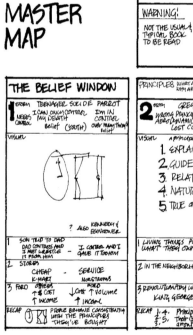

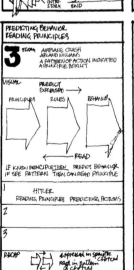

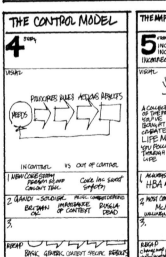

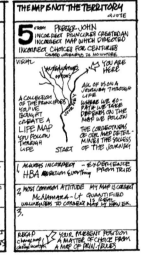

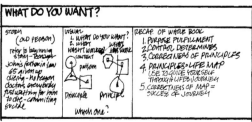

↖ When trying to write a book with two other managers we all were struggling with its content, sequence, and direction, that is until I stayed up into the early hours and visualized its overall sequence into this single diagram.

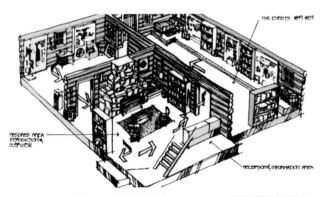

Spatial *Ocean-Coast-Inland, Federal-Local, Metro-politan-Suburban-Rural, Top-Bottom, Inside Outside, Outside-Inside* Maps, travelogues, geographies, and the like follow this spatial sequencing.

Topical *Who, What, When, Where, Why and How, flora, fauna, animal, vegetable, mineral, political, social, philosophical, historical, biological* Most nonfiction books follow a topical sequence, outlining their topics by subject areas.

Motivational *Gain Attention, Build Interest, Create Desire, Spur Action* If your rapid visualizations are driven by marketing you should consider this sequence.

Directed-Eye Preference We all have a natural human tendency to scan images in a predetermined way: top to bottom, left to right, unique to ordinary or just ahead on the path. When I'm laying out any image I'm thinking of this sequence. This one is in your visuals no matter what other sequence that you pick.

Drawings are made to be viewed in a preferred sequence. These sequences can be approximated beforehand and orchestrated deliberately to direct the viewer to more readily see, learn, and accept what you want.

Image Building

The Rapid Drawing of Any Idea

Drawings are built. Fast drawings are built rapidly and simply. I sometimes work as a carpenter, and just as in constructing a house from parts, a drawing is also constructed from parts. With a house it is a 2 X 4 here and a copper pipe there, and with a drawing it's a sphere here and a bold outline there.

This building also happens at various levels. A shape is made from a combination of basic shapes, such as a cylinder and a box. The shapes are placed on to the overall surface of the drawing creating even more com-plex shapes. Value and color is added to the drawing like paint and bricks are added to a building. All of this is working toward to a complete whole.

The more planning and thought you give to what shapes are wanted, how to make those shapes, and where to best place them, the faster and more success-ful your drawing will be.

This drawing of a proposed theme park ride is made from an odd collection of parts.

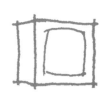

A box becomes a television set which in turn is modified into a huge viewing screen.

This large clear sphere is just a expanded ball. Instead of kicking it you could live inside it.

A modified birthday cake is the central structure.

The foliage is my usual mental rubber stamp.

The railing is just a stretched barbell.

Figures are a collection of indicated figures. Nothing detailed here.

Some of this stuff is made from things I know like bombs and spiders.

More stuff made from whatever I could think of. Just cylinders, half balls, and indicated junk to complete the drawing.

I had to do a little schematic drawing to the side to figure this blasted ride out.

I did this bird's eye view of a section of a city to show some site interrelationships in a meeting. The flat map we were using wasn't working.

This drawing is made from basically only two things: boxes and a waffle.

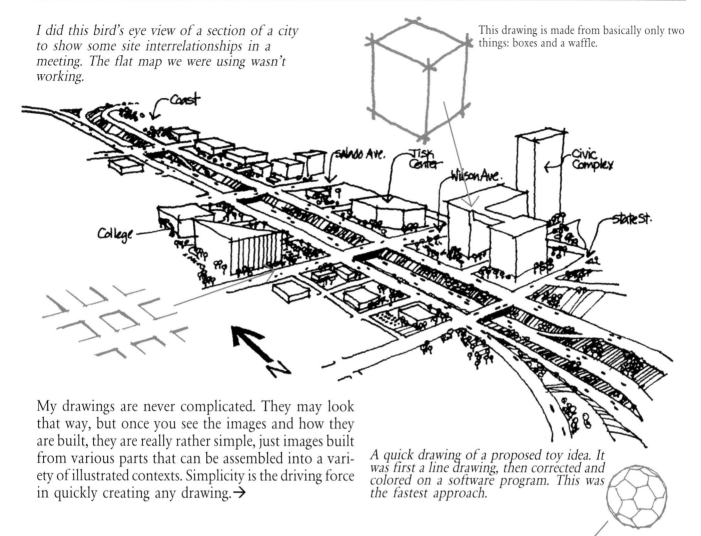

My drawings are never complicated. They may look that way, but once you see the images and how they are built, they are really rather simple, just images built from various parts that can be assembled into a variety of illustrated contexts. Simplicity is the driving force in quickly creating any drawing. →

A quick drawing of a proposed toy idea. It was first a line drawing, then corrected and colored on a software program. This was the fastest approach.

Same ball as on the last page, but used differently.

Same barbell, but now it's a construction toy.

I added some notes and arrows so viewers would have something to hold their attention.

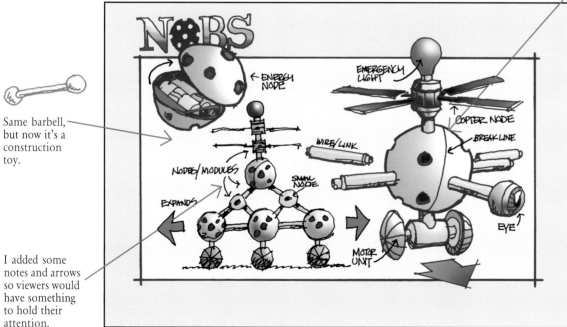

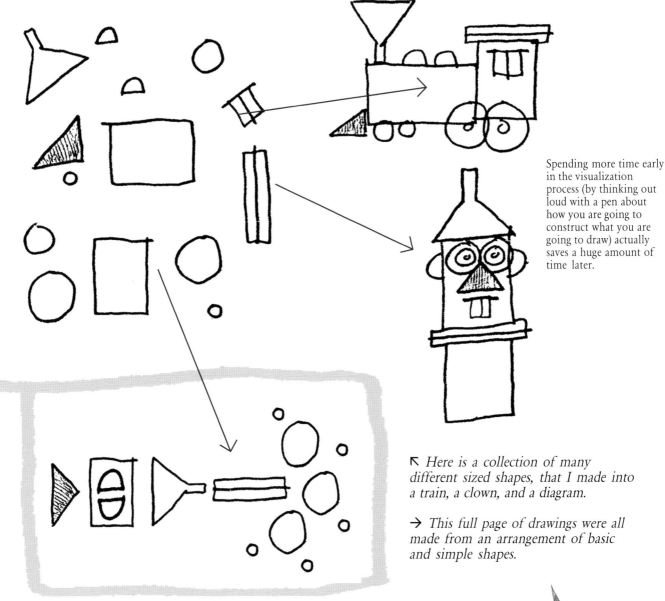

Spending more time early in the visualization process (by thinking out loud with a pen about how you are going to construct what you are going to draw) actually saves a huge amount of time later.

↖ *Here is a collection of many different sized shapes, that I made into a train, a clown, and a diagram.*

→ *This full page of drawings were all made from an arrangement of basic and simple shapes.*

Whenever I'm stuck on a particular part of a drawing and I can't seem to get it to work, I find that reverting back to working only with the basic shapes or parts of the drawing usually helps. The surface of some of the things you have to draw can get very confusing at times. Reverting back to what the images are constructed of removes all the confusing surface stuff and allows you to see the structure of whatever it is you are trying to draw. I find that you can draw complexity better if you start building everything from simplicity.

→ *These witches are made from monster entrails and awful nightmares or were they built from spheres and cones? Were they textured and colored with nasty thoughts and bad intentions or was it a few colored pencils? I can't remember which.*

DR. NINTANI'S
RESTAURANT & HERBATORIUM

These four sketches were all made from simple shapes and the parts of everyday objects. Even the details are still simple shapes, just in ever-decreasing smaller sections of the drawings.

This drawing had to have indicated detail upon detail to give it the feeling that was desired, but it began as a simple assembly of boxes.

WAREHOUSE

CHASE.

TREE'S FACIAL ACTIONS CHOREOGRAPHED TO STORY

MOVING ELEMENTS ON TREE ↓

SOUND EFFECTS
LIGHTED FRUIT

BYSTANDERS WATCHING

PARENTS ALSO GET INVOLVED
ROOT WALL FENCE

STORYTELLER TREE

KIDS INVOLVED IN A STORY

TELESCOPE

DISTANT VIEW

INTERPRETIVE STOP

↑ I SPY LOCATION SIGNAGE

↖ WALKWAY

NOTE: All the sketches above are five inch high felt pen drawings, using line and gray pens on both sides of heavy weight tracing paper.

Image Enhancement

Make Dull Drawings More Exciting

Many drawings fail because they need just a little more effort for them to work. I remember another designer who brought a drawing to me with the plea, "Help me! I don't know what's wrong. Will you show me how to fix it?" When I looked at it, his underlying drawing was fine, better than I could do.

He needed someone with new eyes not jaded by all his work. The goof ball was thinking of throwing the entire drawing away. He didn't see how nice it was under all his overworked efforts to fix it. I took his drawing to a copy machine and made a copy of it on a piece of vellum and then simply worked on enhancing his drawing. It looked great when finished and I made him buy me lunch in payment.

Here are two drawing examples that need to be enhanced a little further using the following techniques.

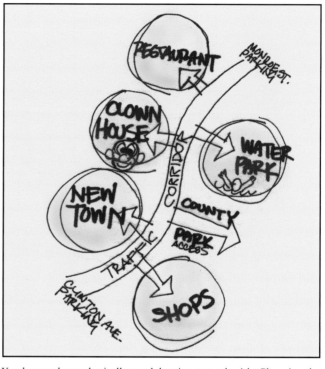

You have to have a basically good drawing to work with. Changing the line weights and adding a little tone is sometimes all that is needed.

↘ *Another designer's unfinished drawing. He didn't have time to complete it and I got the job.*

The original drawing is great. The client made a few changes like removing a roof. What I did from then on was just a bunch of visual tricks.

I first needed to straighten things up. The building was going to collapse if I didn't. I used a straight edge, but a software image program's skew command works too.

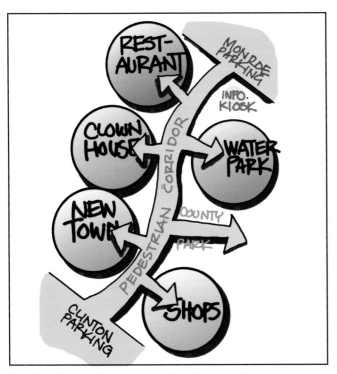

In taking this drawing further I added shadows, color, and contrast. Changing the surfaces from flat to gradation helps.

I then added a bunch of details such as text, shadows, and variations in the tones and colors, stopping before I got too complex.

Basically all I did was vary the line weights and tonal values, especially contrasting the dark areas against the lighter surfaces.

I increased the values between the light and dark tones, using the dark values to feature the structural details. The trees also block the viewer from moving out of the image.

Also, I added more detail to the figures and other selected elements in the drawing. Finally, over all this I added color in overlapping layers.

NOTE: Use figures or parts of figures whenever you can. The viewer identifies with them, and the figures. Pull the viewer into the drawing. The couple above is having an argument.

A Gluelike Hold On Their Attention

Years ago, an art director gave me the following great little tip: "When you have a photo or image on a page, always try to put a caption with it. Your audience will always read it."

This obvious concept works so well that when I've presented my own ideas in competition with others, I've found my ideas have more impact, if only because the viewer spends more time looking at them. They have to. I put little notes all over them, calling out key points, clarifying various elements, and expanding what I'm trying to communicate to them in my sketch, getting them to see more than is really there—more of what they want to see.

Here are some points about notation and lettering I use that may be helpful:

Rule 1 *Any and all copy is always secondary and supportive to the drawings or visual images.*

Rule 2 *Limit any single captions or call-out to no more than a word, phrase, or sentence. More than that bogs things down.*

Rule 3 *Always try to align the copy to the implied or actual hidden grid underneath your page.*

Rule 4 *Use the simple device of lines or arrows to visually link the copy to what it is talking about within the drawing.*

Rule 5 *Keep your lettering simple, easy, and a natural extension of your drawing skill. It isn't worth the effort for anything more than that.*

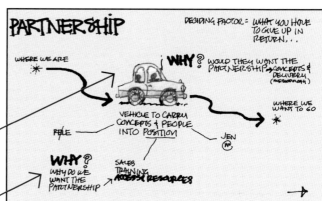

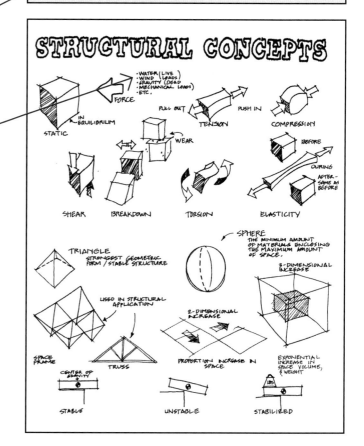

YOU CAN'T GET BLOOD OUT OF A TURNIP.
— COUNT DRACULA

EVERYTHING'S RELATIVE.
— ALBERT EINSTEIN

YOU DON'T HAVE A GHOST OF A CHANCE.
— MACBETH

WELL I'LL BE A MONKEY'S UNCLE!
— CHARLES DARWIN

WITH SIX YOU GET EGGROLL.
— CONFUCIUS

I'M MAD AS HELL AND I'M NOT TAKING
IT ANYMORE!
— RASPUTIN

ANY MAN WHO TAKES TIME WITH HIS JOB
IS OK BY ME.
— ARISTOTLE

COUGH PLEASE.
— HIPPOCRATES

SORRY, I JUST LOST MY HEAD
— MARIE ANTOINETTE

GOT A LIGHT?
— JOAN OF ARC

FOLD, SPINDLE, AND MUTILATE.
— ATTILA THE HUN

WHAT CHERRY TREE?
— GEORGE WASHINGTON

These quotes are about what could have been said and they show how simple my lettering is. My handwriting on the other hand is really impossible to read, another motive for me to print everything.

NOTE

With a simple lettering style your printing can be easily and rapidly modified to generate some interest. For example, with a line at the end of each letter you can make it into a serif faced letter like the one above. Slant the lettering and you make your printing into an italic face. By changing the weight of the pen used, you have a bold face head or a light face caption. Using simple lettering keeps any drawing notation moving rapidly towards completion. Anymore than that, and it's faster, better, and easier to use a computer.

Work Faster By Working Smaller

More than any other single visualization approach I know, many problems can be solved faster, and solutions generated quicker, by working smaller. Doing a drawing small makes you work faster because there isn't much to what you are drawing. You can't get bogged down in all the details because there aren't any details. You have to work on the overall image, the idea, and its placement because there isn't anything but those things to work with.

I especially like doing thumbnail drawings when I first start on a project because of a trick they do with the mind. When working really small the brain has to interpret and infuse meaning into what these little squiggles and lines mean. It is like the drawing shifts to inside my head. An easy and clear dialog occurs between the thumbnail and the mind, uncluttered by the usual noise of techniques, materials, and skill levels. No other visualization tool I know of can create such an intimate conversation with an idea as a thumbnail drawing.

They call these little drawings thumbnails because they are small, about the size of your thumbnail. I don't know about you, but my thumbnails aren't this big.

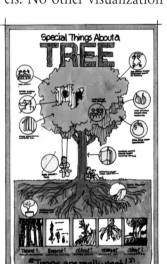

It is often easier to solve larger problems with a drawing by first working much smaller.

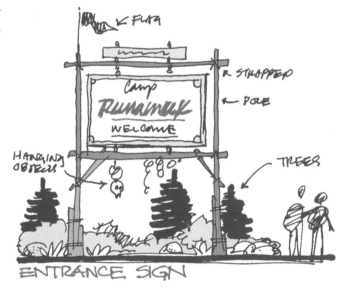

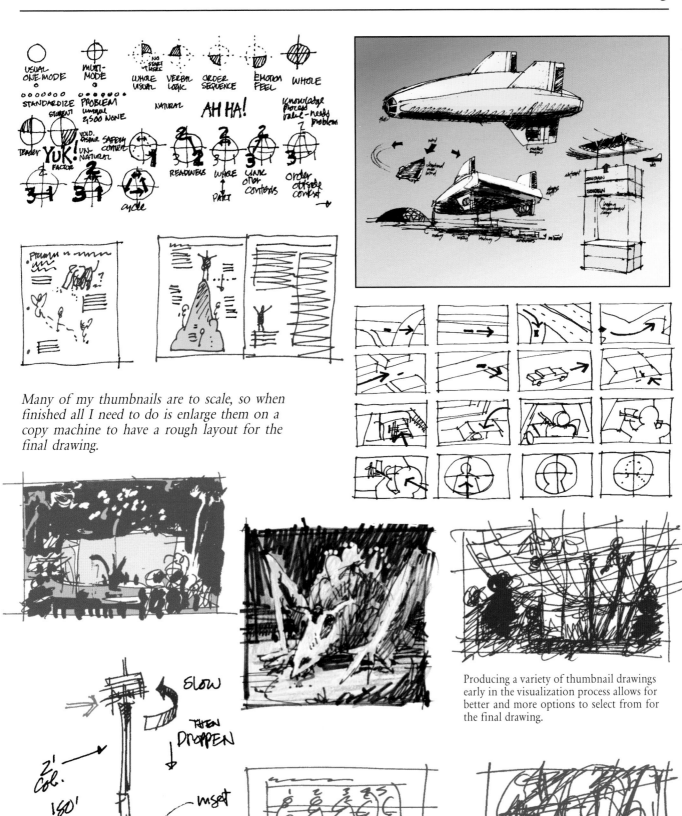

Many of my thumbnails are to scale, so when finished all I need to do is enlarge them on a copy machine to have a rough layout for the final drawing.

Producing a variety of thumbnail drawings early in the visualization process allows for better and more options to select from for the final drawing.

Content Scribing

Visualizing Meaning

Design is thought of as the aesthetic optimization of form, space, or sequence. But if you look a little deeper, design concerns itself with the enhancement of the human interaction through tools, shelters, processes, and content. If you look still deeper it also concerns itself with the enhancement of meaning and understanding.

One of the best tools for this enhancement of meaning is the visual construction of representational structures. This is never more evident that when a designer/

artist visually and symbolically reflects back to someone what that person is saying. That is at the heart of *Content Scribing.*

In Content Scribing the information given at a presentation or generated in a meeting is visually noted in full view of all involved. These quickly drawn images on a board become a collective notebook, dramatically focusing attention on the evolving visual content.

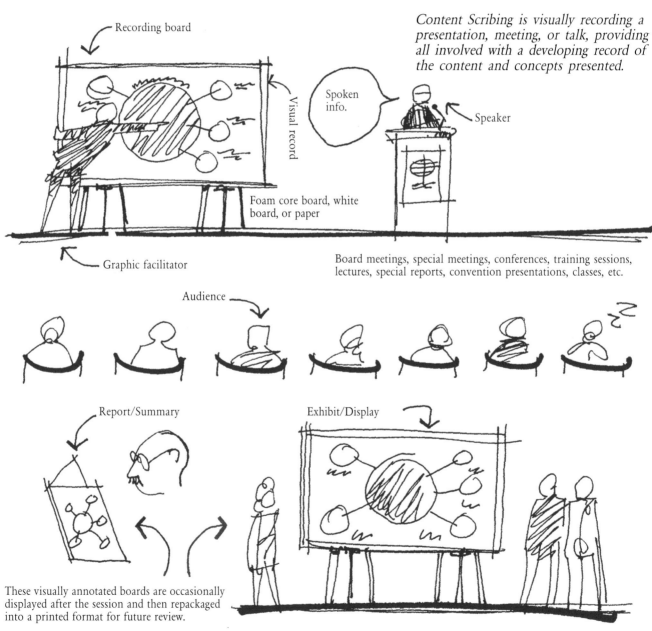

Content Scribing is visually recording a presentation, meeting, or talk, providing all involved with a developing record of the content and concepts presented.

Recording board

Spoken info.

Speaker

Visual record

Foam core board, white board, or paper

Graphic facilitator

Board meetings, special meetings, conferences, training sessions, lectures, special reports, convention presentations, classes, etc.

Audience

Report/Summary

Exhibit/Display

These visually annotated boards are occasionally displayed after the session and then repackaged into a printed format for future review.

NOTE: Content Scribing can easily become the day's entertainment. When this becomes its driving purpose you will then have to assume the role of performer. Some visualizers like this. I'm not one of them.

In Content Scribing the visualizer assumes the roll of secretary or court reporter, playing a non-intrusive facilitator role by creating images with captions that capture the essential meaning of what is going on.

A Content Scribing Example

You may find yourself dead center in all sorts of un-anticipated situations when scribing. In one corporate meeting I was asked to *"make some pictures for them."* The meeting began with a thud of immediate frustration and anxiety in everyone there. First one person then another would bring up separate issues.

I was totally lost until I saw the need for a map that showed the progress of this firm through time, linking everybody's comments into some sort of cohesive whole. The minute the map appeared all the people in the meeting started inserting into it what was important to them. The comments came fast and furious. I didn't have time to think, just to capture the information as fast as I could. Everyone was standing. *They had gone through the birth and death, then rebirth of their company and simply wanted it to count for something in their exciting future.*

What happened after this meeting was very interesting. Before people seemed lost and unsure of themselves—after the map appeared the opposite happened. With one central image everyone in the room had an icon that created a cohesive shared vision of their future.

The image I made was a mess; not anything like the one you see on the right. Only the participants could see and understand it. In order to share this map with others in the company I redrew the version you see.

Making The Best Use of Experience

Some designers like to perform impressive magic tricks. They have people in the office gather around them. Then, while seated on a stool with a sheet of paper in front of them, these designers begin to draw, astounding their fellow workers with their abilities. A deft stroke here, a quick image built there, and all with such unwavering ease. But I know their tricks. What they are drawing, they have drawn many times before. So many times, in fact, that the procedure to draw it has been permanently infused in their brain cells. It has reached the level of becoming subliminal and automatic. What they are doing in these performances is essentially to dump visual cliches in front of their mesmerized onlookers.

When any designer or artist finishes the drawing they are working on, something from that drawing remains inside their heads for the next drawing. After years of collecting these images quite a few of these drawing cliches have built up, stuffing the visual closets full in their minds. We all pretend they aren't there and that each design is unique, but it isn't. Each design drawing is often mostly a collection of cliches. Sure, there is the part of the drawing that is unique. There has to be. The uniqueness of the context makes it so. The exact arrangement of the drawing may be very different that any done before. But what is unique and applicable to the context of the drawing and what do you have that is left over? Just similar images that have been repeatedly sketched and resketched. →

I have hundreds of rubber stamp-like images like these stuck in my mind. I use them to lighten my work load so I can focus on the truly unique ideas within a drawing.

I use mentally filed away images to quickly rubber stamp the majority of the work on many drawings. It is the best way to achieve the needed speed.

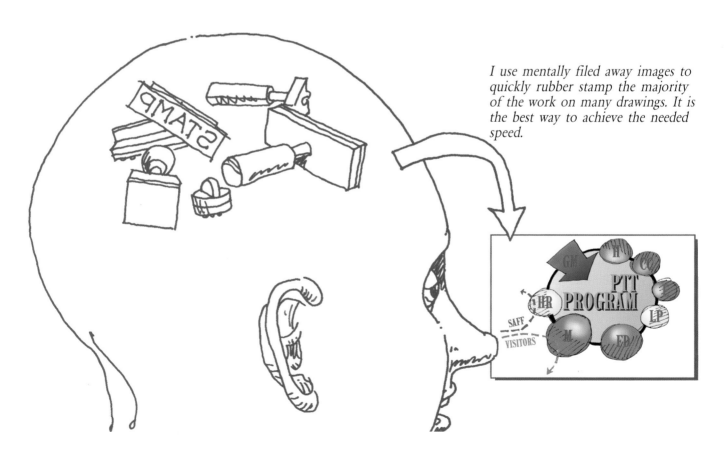

 ←*One little architectural concept stuck in a closet of my mind is a series of overlapping roofs. Shown here are two seemingly different drawings for two entirely different clients using that very same mental rubber-stamped building concept.*

The secret is out. But in keeping with the purpose of this book, I feel that I finally must admit something. *Every new drawing is an eclectic collection of every other drawing and every other image its artist or designer has created since they first touched pen to paper.*

Awareness and acceptance of this natural process is a great source of material to be effectively used on your next drawing. Making this process both conscious and deliberate saves time and effort. It's done anyway, just admit it. This can greatly lighten your load when doing any drawing. We all build up an incredible collection of mental images, filling up a huge visual data bank, that we can access at a moment's notice. Cliches have their value in life, even drawing cliches.

Let me tell you another little story. I was working for a company where I had to continually show a steady stream of demanding clients two alternative designs.

One thing I used many times on this drawing as visual filler are overlapping light and dark layers.

Drawings like the one below can get so complicated that only by focusing on what is truly unique and standardizing the rest could I hope to get it done fast.

Does this roof look familiar?

A rubber-stamped mental image here, another over there, and still more right here.

I first blocked this drawing in using the ultimate of cliches, a bunch of boxes, then filled it with stuff I've used many times before.

That takes double the work because I always had to come up with two designs on two separate drawings. So I decided to do something about this and actually talked marketing into going along with me.

I created an obvious reject, full of silly cliches that the only thing the client could do was to reject it. This allowed me to spend more time on improving the drawing of the best design. Sure enough, the client did the expected and commandingly rejected our planted reject and picked the better design. This approach worked out just great until the day came when our most important client thought our planted reject was the best solution. *You can take a great technique too far.*

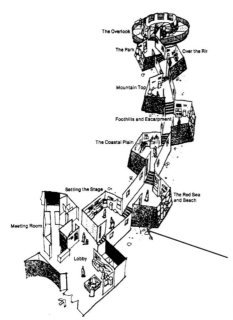

More drawings full of mental rubber stamps:

When drawing a visual synopsis of some knowledge, using this approach is mandatory. People need standard visual symbols to interpret the visualization correctly.

The basic structure of this Saudi Arabian Center is unique, but everything else is only a collection of standardized images.

A common box is made into a refrigerator. The edging details and shading are standard. It's only in the arrangement of those elements where the unique design is.

NOTE: Use your growing collection of mental images as building modules to plug into your drawing as it is being constructed.

Make Your Drawings Come Alive

The human figure gives life to any drawing. Figures pull anyone into the images on the paper and involves them in what is being presented. People identify with other people even when those people are drawn with a simple line. Drawn people serve a proxies for those viewing the sketches.

But the human figure is one of the most complicated subjects to draw. It's a good thing that with rapid design drawings it is not necessary to draw the figure in any great detail. An indication of the figure will work very effectively. Capture just enough of the human form to help the viewer identify with your drawings.

Placing figures in groups creates a natural look.

Many of my figures are derived from a square and the faces are simply indicated.

The unit of measurement is one square.

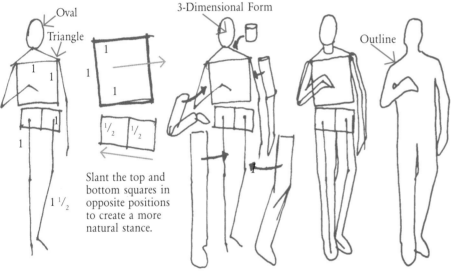

Oval

Triangle

3-Dimensional Form

Outline

Slant the top and bottom squares in opposite positions to create a more natural stance.

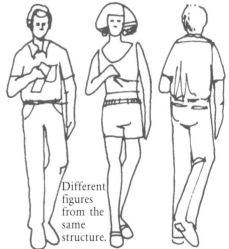

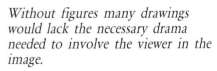

Different figures from the same structure.

Indicated figures help drawings communicate a desired attitude, feeling, or atmosphere.

Figures pull the viewer looking at your drawing into the design. They help them see themselves inside your design.

Without figures many drawings would lack the necessary drama needed to involve the viewer in the image.

Female figures have more rounded and slimmer forms. Male figures have bolder and more square forms. Kids have different proportions than adults, such as having bigger heads in relation to their bodies.

The same
structure
for both
figures.

Have your figures doing typical actions of people such as sitting, talking, leaning, bending, and holding things. Avoid extreme actions that pull attention away from what you want the viewer to focus on.

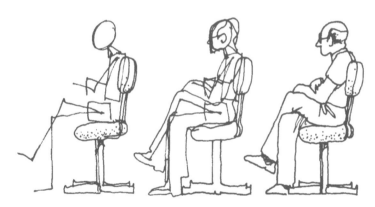

Figures are some of the most effective devices you can use to establish scale for whatever is featured in the drawing.

Pull the viewer into your drawings by helping them see themselves as doing the same things the people are doing.

Specific functions can be clearly communicated with the careful placement of figures doing certain specific actions.

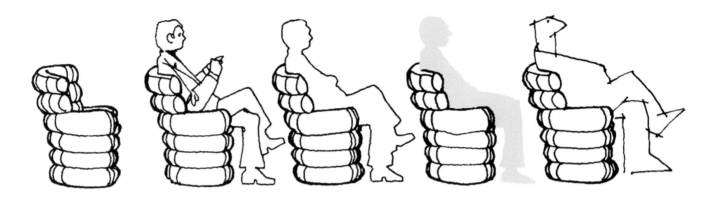

Indicating The Human Form The Easy Way

Figures in a drawing act as a standard of measurement to establish scale. Figures, or parts of figures, define the activity being represented in the drawing better than anything else.

How the figure is drawn is sometimes not important. The fact that it is drawn may be critical to the drawing achieving its intended purpose.

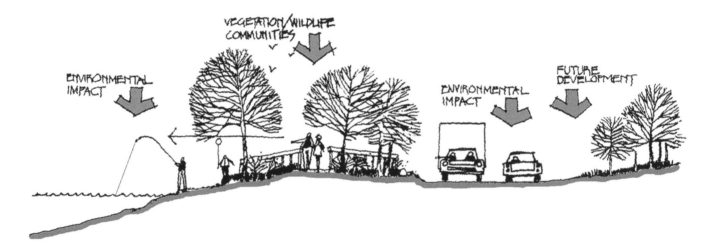

Even in the rough stages of a drawing that no one sees, I place figures in it to help me in putting myself into the drawing.

Without the simple black silhouette of the person in this drawing it would lose much of what it is trying to communicate.

Parts of the human figure work at clarifying drawings. Hands are hard to draw, so I have someone pose for me.

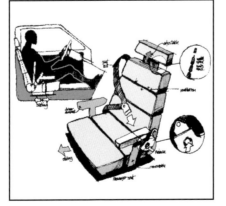

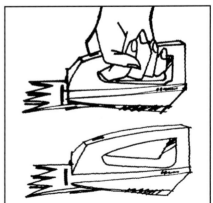

NOTE: When placing figures in a drawing have them looking at whatever it is you want the viewer to also see. It makes them look, too. Also, don't have a figure stare at the viewer. Staring makes everyone nervous.

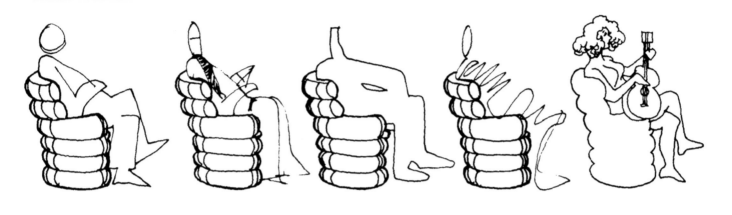

NOTE: I've used all the ways you see here in drawing the human figure. At first, I used to think about how to construct the figure I was drawing, but now I've done it so many times it has become automatic.

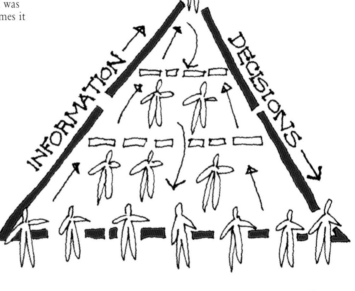

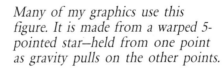

Figures with a little personality can work better, but be careful to not make them more interesting than what you are illustrating.

Many of my graphics use this figure. It is made from a warped 5-pointed star—held from one point as gravity pulls on the other points.

This is my favorite kind of lightning fast figure. Usually it's enough.

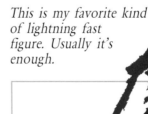

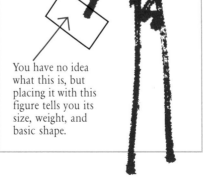

You have no idea what this is, but placing it with this figure tells you its size, weight, and basic shape.

Scale-Up Solutions

Solving Problems Before They Arrive

Scale-up is a process I developed some years ago, and it has earned me more odd looks and wry smiles than any other visual technique I use. When other designers first see these small drawings they always laugh. But laughs switch to smiles and then into astonishment and curiosity. It does seem an odd thing to do—develop a drawing or visual presentation in miniature. But it works.

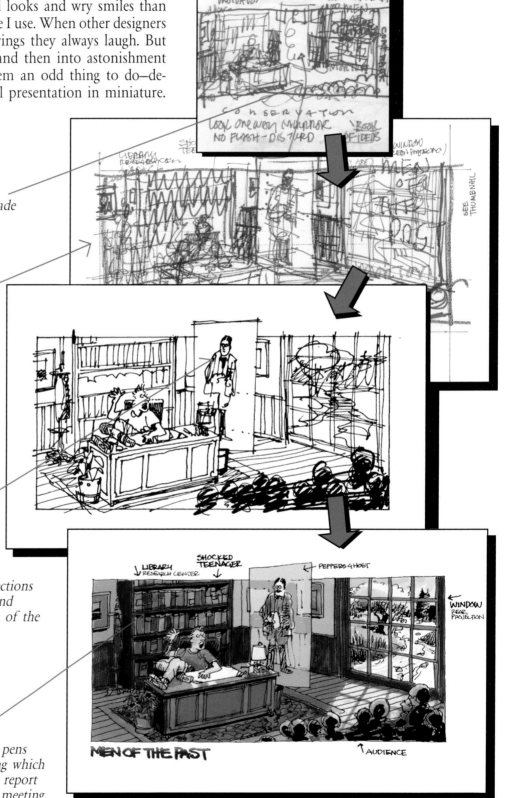

1 A thumbnail sketch made on a Post-It Note® is roughly to scale.

2 Next a rough drawing on tracing paper is made over a greatly enlarged copy of the little drawing.

3 A drawing is done on transparent vellum over the top of the previous drawing.

Corrections are made with a white-out pen or sections of the image are redrawn and pasted over corrected parts of the original.

4 Gray and colored felt pens create the final drawing which can be used in both a report and a formal presentation meeting.

SPECIAL NOTE: When I hand-color my drawings I first use gray felt pens until I have a completed grey toned image, then I color the drawings with my color felt pens. Coloring this way increases the variety of color and the depth to the final drawings.

When I'm finished with these small drawings I go to a copy machine and enlarge them exactly to size.

Working large allows many things to go on because you can see too much. It is very easy to get bogged down too soon in the hairy details when working large. Everything slows down. But with these small drawings you can't get hung up on the details—you can't even see them.

Small scale drawings done in the beginning phases of a project remind you to put only what you need to concentrate on in front of you. You can only focus on the overall look of your drawing. Then when you

enlarge these diminutive drawings on the copy machine, the details automatically appear at just the right point of the developmental process. Scale-up forces the mind to do the appropriate design and drawing activity at just the right time.

Also, something magical happens in the dark corners of the mind when using this process. I believe it forces details out of the way and focuses the creative mind, allowing it to have a more holistic and effective dialog with developing ideas.

Actual Size *for a set of thumbnails done for an entire book.*

One-Fifth Scale *of the final matching pages for the finished book.*

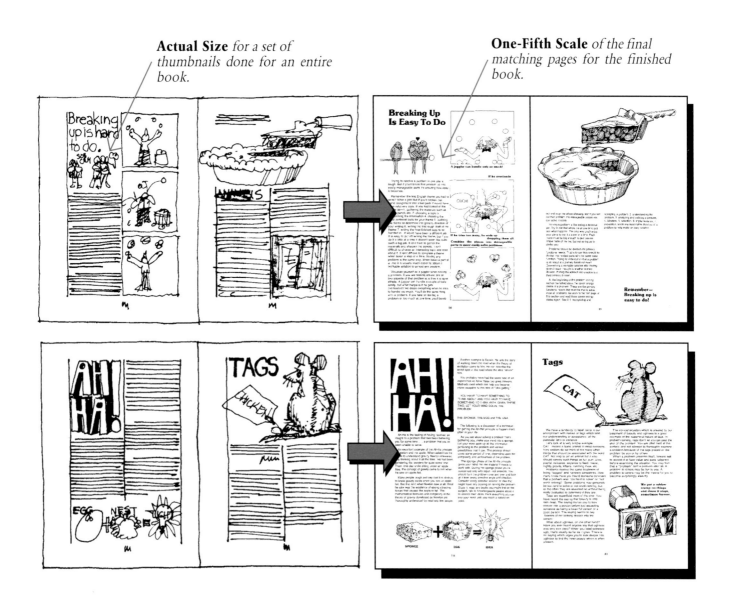

When Doing More Drawings Is Easier

My drawings never seem to be right the first time around. They always have mistakes in them. I do think a perfect drawing could happen the first time. (I have heard a rumor of an architect in Cleveland who did one back in the 1980s.)

When I begin a drawing, it is always off in some way.

I have to evolve and refine the drawing as I go along. The early rough lines and forms on cheap paper give me the needed visual feedback for what I should do next. Then I redraw parts or all of the drawing, correcting and improving as I go.

Evolving a drawing usually involves one of these two approaches:

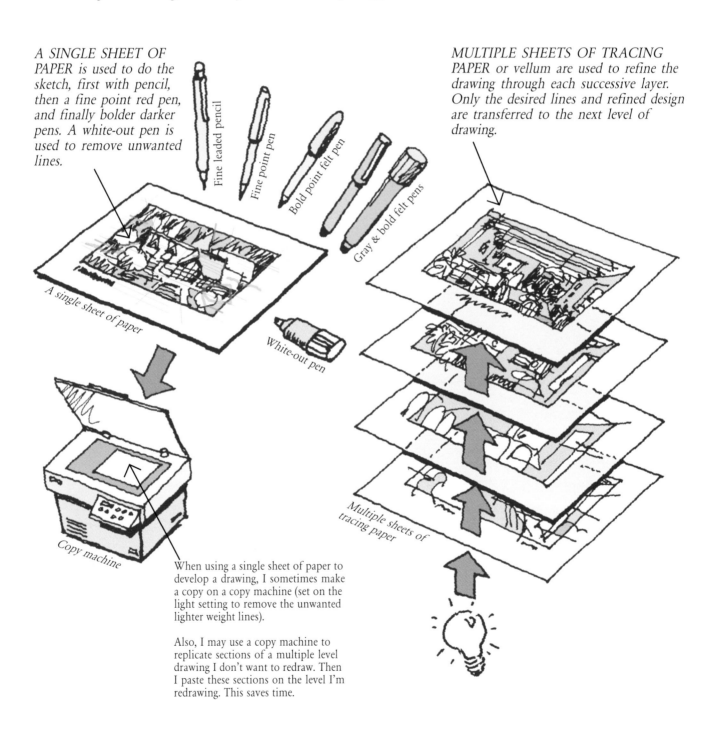

A SINGLE SHEET OF PAPER is used to do the sketch, first with pencil, then a fine point red pen, and finally bolder darker pens. A white-out pen is used to remove unwanted lines.

Fine leaded pencil

Fine point pen

Bold point felt pen

Gray & bold felt pens

A single sheet of paper

White-out pen

Copy machine

MULTIPLE SHEETS OF TRACING PAPER or vellum are used to refine the drawing through each successive layer. Only the desired lines and refined design are transferred to the next level of drawing.

Multiple sheets of tracing paper

When using a single sheet of paper to develop a drawing, I sometimes make a copy on a copy machine (set on the light setting to remove the unwanted lighter weight lines).

Also, I may use a copy machine to replicate sections of a multiple level drawing I don't want to redraw. Then I paste these sections on the level I'm redrawing. This saves time.

Occasionally this Evolutionary Drawing process is just not as sequential and clean as one would like it to be. Design drawing often involves working with other people where things can get very complicated and messy. As a consequence, many evolving drawings are pushed into unanticipated directions.

For example, the drawing below began on a napkin at lunch. Then it went into a computer using a CAD program. Finally it was redrawn into a sketched drawing. This was the fastest, easiest, and least expensive approach. The fact that I had used a CAD program, in the client's mind, made it more expensive. So I never told him. →

1 The first step in this modified evolutionary process was a scribbled note on a napkin over a lunch meeting.

2 The next step was a drawing done using a $25 CAD system (honest!) that I bought at a discount store. This computer drawing worked well at quickly laying out the perspective.

3 Finally, I overlaid a sheet of tracing paper and roughed out a final rough sketch for the client of a proposed store design.

Evolutionary Drawing

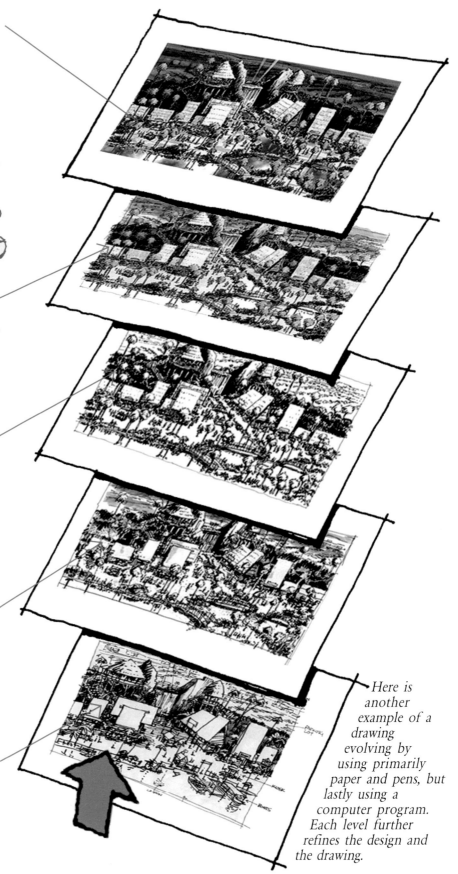

5 *The previously hand colored drawing was scanned into a computer. The color was softened and enhanced. Then a reflective sky in the water was put in with a simple keystroke in a drawing program.*

I use a computer to draw whenever it is better and faster to do so.

4 *This drawing is done with colored pencil on a copy of the previous line drawing. The surface texture of bond paper is better to color on than tracing paper.*

3 *I sometimes completely redraw the drawing on vellum in felt tip fine point line to clean it up. This step is often unnecessary.*

2 *Only those places needing change or correction on the drawing are redrawn and then pasted on a copy of the original. This corrected copy is then recopied.*

1 *A beginning rough drawing on tracing paper using a fine point and a couple of warm gray felt pens.*

Here is another example of a drawing evolving by using primarily paper and pens, but lastly using a computer program. Each level further refines the design and the drawing.

Even though working with other people can slow down your rapid visualization, you can use their input and insight to make your drawing better.

In the evolving drawing below, the first ideas were just talked about. A rough line drawing was then done on tracing paper. This drawing was faxed far and wide.

When everyone was finally through with their input, the drawing was finished and then scanned into a computer. The actual drawing took only a few hours to do, but all the input and corrections from others stretched those hours into days. Below is only part of all this input on my evolving drawings for this project.

CLIENT We need to show a jungle type of ride that will travel the park's perimeter. I also want a crashed airplane in the drawing that a visitor can see from the boat. I can't send you a site plan-it isn't done yet.

ME Here is the rough sketch of the jungle ride. (Faxed)

CLIENT Yes, it looks good. I have a photo of a beautiful sky (in Kansas) I think it has the right colors for the sky in this drawing. (E-mailed)

ME Here is the concept drawing with a Kansas sky.

CLIENT Great, except there is no way they will like the skulls or Easter Island heads. Try using what you suggested earlier and a tiki god.

CLIENT The black and white version of this drawing works suprisingly well in the report and press kit. Also, I had a copy center print a 24 X 36 inch copy of the color version and it looks great.

CLIENT How did you do that reflection?

ME I just used the mask, flip, copy, and paste functions in a computer imaging program. (Photoshop®)

RULE ONE of Evolutionary Drawing is never replicate a drawing or part of a drawing by hand if you can use a copy machine. Make a copy of whatever you're just replicating by hand, cut it out, and then place it on the next level you're working on—it's faster.

Stuff Indication

Capture Its Essence In A Few Strokes

Most design drawings are overdrawn. It is easy to overdraw a drawing. You fall in love with some part of it, refine and polish it, taking it to a point where the drawing has become an end in itself.

A design drawing is always a means to some end. Its purpose is to communicate a future design to the people needing to see what a proposed project will look like. Taking drawing beyond a certain point may ac-

tually thwart this purpose. Keeping a minimal use of line, tone, detail, and color in your drawings involves the viewer in the process of seeing. Holding back to indicate just the bare essentials of parts of your drawing allows the viewer to become a active participant by putting into the drawing what they think is there.

Here are the major techniques I use in indicating all the stuff that make up my drawings:

1 **Use A Minimal Amout of Linework** *Try using only enough lines to describe what is necessary, especially with the background or with supportive material.*

All the pine trees are the same tree reduced to its descriptive essence and placed where needed.

Both roof lines are the same, drawn more as a flat graphic element than in perspective.

Just an overlapping pattern of outdoor seating, letting the mind fill in the details.

Indicated figures repeatedly placed in the drawing.

2 **Describe Only The Key Elements** *Everything you draw has certain key features that are critical to visually describing it. It may be a surface pattern, a corner junction, or a structural essence. Make sure you draw those elements, indicating the rest of the drawing with as few lines as possible.*

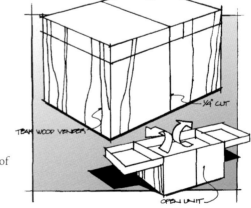

The key elements of this box are the corners and edges.

Save time by picking the most descriptive view.

FOOD CART

Drawing only the shadows completes the whole trees.

3 Pick The Best View *Select a view of whatever you're drawing that best describes it. A view that features what you want to show to the best advantage in transferring more meaning, easier.*

5 Draw The Shade and Shadows First *Try working from dark to light in your drawings. First draw its darkest shadows, then proceed into the light until you reach that point where the drawing shifts into a completed image.*

4 Capture Its Essential Character *Everying you draw has a essential icon-like outline that communicates its meaning. Often, only drawing that with a few lines is all that is needed.*

6 Use Situational Cliches *You can utilize the visual cliches contained in our shared cultural memory. Save your more involved drawing efforts on those things you want to feature or that are unique.*

Any drawing is just a collection of shapes, lines, and colors that symbolically represent meaning. A drawing is never the thing or interaction it represents, but always a representation. The artist/designer assigns meaning to the various parts of their drawing in the hope that a similar meaning will be triggered within the mind of their intended audience.

I remember what an illustrator said to me years ago,

"You know, your drawings make little sense as you work on them. Your lines are not even straight. You're too lazy to get off your rear and find a ruler. Plus, if I look at any part of your drawing, I haven't the slightest idea what it is. But when you're finally finished, everything comes together and you really do give a clear impression of what you're trying to show." I'm always trying for this overall impression from the viewer by using the following few steps:

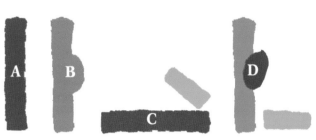

Certain shapes are predetermined by the viewer. A block of Swiss cheese has to be triangular with holes, for example. But many shapes you use in your drawings are entirely up to you.

1 Select The Appropriate Shapes *Meaningfully link to your audience's world. Some of the shapes (with their color, tone, and texture) are set and predetermined, but with some of the shapes the only thing that matters is that they assist in achieving the overall desired impression.*

← *Here is an silly little example of the assignment of meaning to shapes:*
A. Your Dad B. Your Mom, as she tells your Dad that she is pregnant with you. C. Your Dad's reaction, with the dog trying to revive him. D. You (you look like your Dad), your Mom, and the dog. Dad has gone to work to pay for you.

2 Establish Scale For The Shapes *Put the selected shape into an interaction with other identifiable shapes to set the size of the shape. Often, what is put in association with a shape is more important that the shape itself.*

← *The rectangle could be any size or scale when it is out there all alone. But when it is put into contact with known and recognizable shapes, the rectangle suddenly has an established size.*

It is just a rectangle until it is place next to another recognized shape and then something happens.

The association between shapes is more important that the shapes themselves. This where the meaning is located.

3 Indicate Key Elements With The Shapes *Everything in this world has some part of it that if left out wouldn't allow you to recognize what it was. Make sure your shapes include crucial descriptive elements included.*

A box is just that until you include a few descriptive elements and then the box becomes something else. →

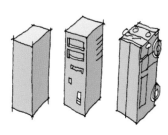

4 **Assemble The Shapes Into An Overall Impression** *There is a trick I use on my students. I show them one of my completed and mounted drawings and they usually stroke my ego with ohs and ahs until I then cover my drawing with paper until only a small section is all that shows. Then I point to the exposed section and ask "Could you draw that?" "Sure I can," is the answer.*

I have them draw the little section; they usually show me up. At that point I ask another question, "What makes the difference then between your drawings and mine?" The difference is in the assembly of all those parts and shapes. Some people spend far too much time on how to draw shapes instead of how to assemble and arrange those shapes into meaningful responses. This is where a great savings in effort and the magic lies.

These shapes often don't make much sense unless viewed in their location within the entire drawing.

Any part of these rapidly visualized settings is simple. Just look close and you will see what I mean. There is nothing that is very complicated or very sophisticated.

Look closely at these shapes. Anything complex here? Just simple indicated shapes that are assembled and arranged into giving the desired impression.

A Visual Tool for Capturing Ideas

The class I disliked the most in high school was English and the thing that I disliked the most was diagramming sentences. The teacher was an old stern spinster with a constipation problem. I never got sentence diagramming right, but then again, I never got anything right in her class. So when the concept of diagramming ideas was first proposed to me I had an immediate strong aversion to it. A writer showed me and then taught me this process and it has proven itself a godsend. Once he got it through my head why I needed it, I've used this technique extensively ever since.

Basically it is a simple process, easy to learn and very easy to use. A few simple lines, each having a word or two written on it, capture the ideas being presented in a book, a meeting, a lecture, or whatever form ideas are being communicated.

It is basically like a tree. A trunk is the main idea, then limbs coming out of the trunk are the main supporting ideas, and finally any material for those supporting ideas branch out from there.

It is called by any number of names, but the term *Content Map* is the one I've always liked. It is the name for what it does. Also, I've noticed over the years many people trying to make it complicated, but it just isn't. The reason for Content Mapping's effectiveness and speed is because of this underlying simplicity.

This is your basic Content Map. Any other map that you will ever see, no matter the colors, shapes, and images used is essentially this same basic structure.

Every idea has its place. You can quickly see where it belongs and how other ideas relate to it.

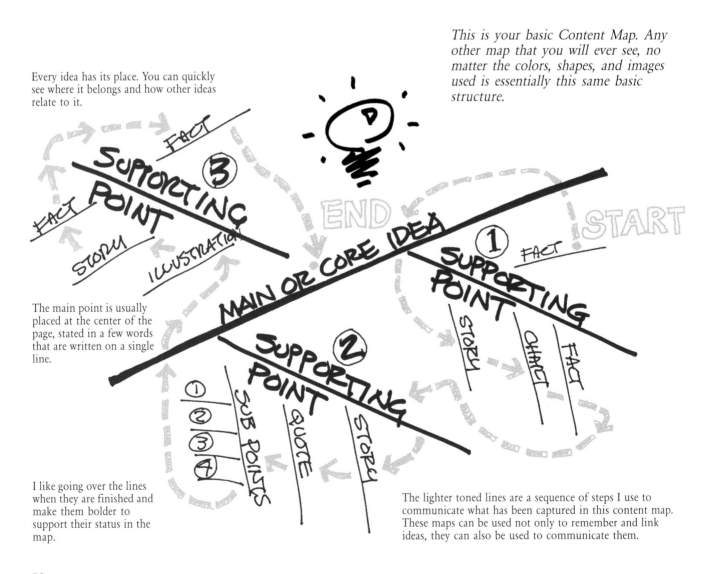

The main point is usually placed at the center of the page, stated in a few words that are written on a single line.

I like going over the lines when they are finished and make them bolder to support their status in the map.

The lighter toned lines are a sequence of steps I use to communicate what has been captured in this content map. These maps can be used not only to remember and link ideas, they can also be used to communicate them.

Content Mapping also has a bit of magic in it. There has been many times where I've used it to capture a conversation or presentation from someone. (It is the fastest way that I know of to capture ideas, concepts, or facts into a cohesive structure so I use this tool all the time.) Then, after I capture this person's content and it lies out in front of me on a single page, their ideas fit together better than when they originally presented the material. When I then present the information, I often find its originator taking notes. I've even had them ask me, "Where did you get those ideas" or "These ideas are similar to what I've been thinking, but more developed and much clearer than mine." I've given up trying to tell them they are their ideas. They won't believe me.

Content Mapping rapidly makes ideas into a visual structure where everything has to fit and be interconnected in order to stand and link together. Ideas and concepts are thus made more cohesive and clear. You can see at a single glance where every idea fits. It's one great visual information capturing tool. Maybe that old spinster English teacher had an important point after all.

This is a map I created after reading a good book on visual language.

I find that quickly scanning this map brings everthing back to my mind even after years have passed since first content mapping this information.

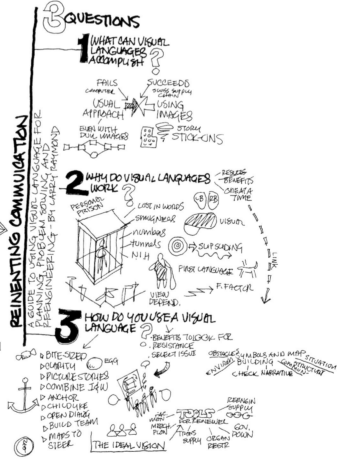

I also use this tool to get a handle on the information being presented in the various meetings that I have to attend.

Content maps not only capture a meeting's important content they also show how chaotic and disjointed most meetings usually are.

Storyboarding

**Small Scale Sequential Visualizations
of Large Scale Projects**

A storyboard is a series of little sketches made before a film begins shooting to help sequence and design individual shots and scenes. *Storyboarding* is used to inexpensively see on paper what is needed before the costly production process begins. Storyboards are used in creating animation, television commercials, game design, and multimedia projects. But they can be used wherever you need to conceptualize, see, design, and plan a sequence of activities.

Typically, the written script to a movie is done first. From this script, sketches are made with each drawing being a shot. Then each series of sequential sketches becomes a scene until a visual outline of the entire film can be seen.

Though originating in film, the creative application of storyboards is increasingly expanding into many new areas such as negotiation, user interface, innovative thinking, web page design, and product development.

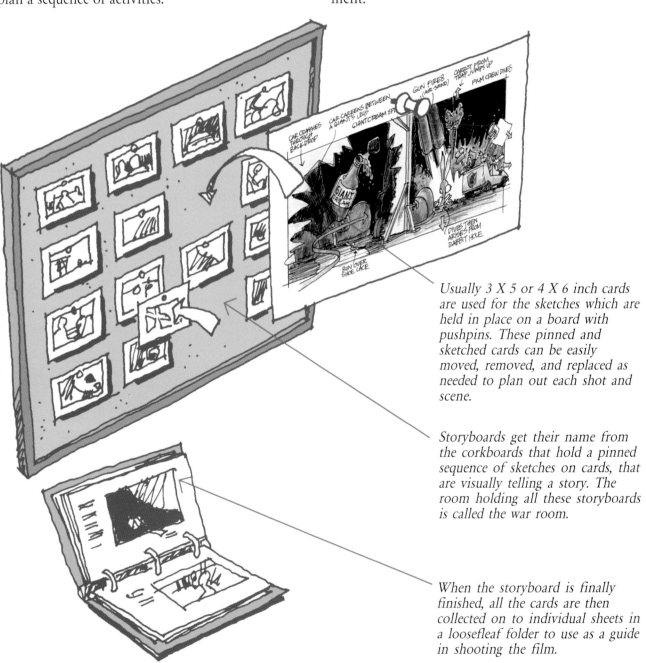

Usually 3 X 5 or 4 X 6 inch cards are used for the sketches which are held in place on a board with pushpins. These pinned and sketched cards can be easily moved, removed, and replaced as needed to plan out each shot and scene.

Storyboards get their name from the corkboards that hold a pinned sequence of sketches on cards, that are visually telling a story. The room holding all these storyboards is called the war room.

When the storyboard is finally finished, all the cards are then collected on to individual sheets in a loosefleaf folder to use as a guide in shooting the film.

I first learned to use storyboards back when I was working as an assistant art director for a motion picture company. Though I've used storyboards when creating and communicating the concepts for a film, I more often use a storyboard to easily and quickly show a sequence of views a person would see moving through a space that has yet to be built.

Storyboarding allows me to generate the conceptualized frames of view a person visiting a proposed theme park would experience, seeing a new exhibit expansion in a museum, or walking through a retail store's expansion before it has even been built. In situations like these, I've never found a better method for showing yourself and others what it's like to travel through all sorts of physical possibilities. →

Selections from a storyboard showing the design of the sequence of events occurring during a theme park ride.

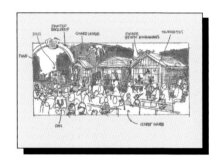
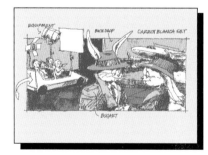

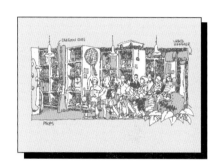

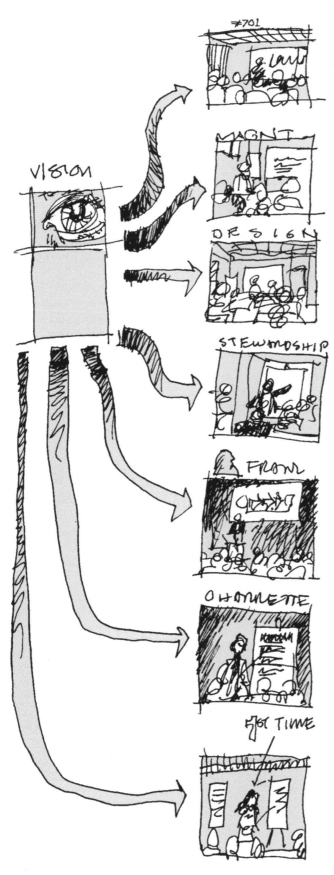

There is another place where storyboarding isn't normally used, though it's an extremely effective tool. It's in ideating and sequencing instructional design and business training.

All teaching is sequential and my kind of instruction is primarily visual. This is an ideal match for storyboarding. This tool's little pictures help in packaging the content into frames or pages with supporting graphics and stories to accurately see the whole approach before investing time, money, and other limited resources. This quickly and cheaply solves problems and refines direction of my concepts. It allows me test out my instructional ideas, or any other ideas, before any major commitment is demanded in further development of those ideas.

In all of these areas, these little drawings solve more problems, generate more really great ideas, and save more money that just about any other rapid visualization technique you could use.

←A notebook page where I was using a modified storyboard to plan some future alternative directions.

→Examples of storyboards, going counter clockwise from the top left: concepts for a short movie, a visualized movie script, a public service commercial, and a proposed TV station renovation.

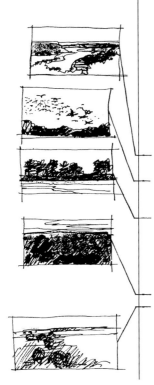

2

The growing river twists its way through the high plains as it charts a course in natural splendor. Myriad forad of wildlife in natural state render the scene complete; symbiotic relationsips crystalized. Back to the river, always back to the river. Cutting from one scene back to a river scene reinforces the movement Of time, and nature, towards a rendezvous with human aspirations. Music heightens the appreciation for the tranquility and the harmony of the great plains and its denizens. Buffalo, woodchucks, prairie dogs birds all are shown unhurried and oblivious to imminent change.

BAD DREAMS
78

LILITH: (Whispering) Down the attempt by the others, Kog. I've gotten through! *She touches the control; first the image haltingly appears. Then fills the entire wall with an image of the two investigators talking. Adjusting the control knobs, she begins to hear their voices.*
KOG: (Yelling at here over the ear phones) You've gotten through? You've gotten thought! Please, please tell me you've found them!
LILITH: (Loudly whispering) Shut up! Yes, I see them. They do know each other. Liar, liar, pants on fire. They are talking like old friends. . . . . give me just a second and I'll tune this so I can hear them. Gradually

Lilith has finally turned on the viewer and located Dameon and Scott. Their are talking at the edge of an elevated parking overhang.

the voices come into hearing range and you can hear them nervously chatting.
KOG: (Hesitantly) . . . what are the-they saying?
LILITH: Not much. Just how-ya-doin kind of talk. But they are together. They know each other well like old friends shoot'n the bull. Wait, wait, quiet they are saying something that may be important. *The sound of the voices increases to what they are saying can be clearly made out. Suddenly, the voices and the image of the two banks out and a huge face appears.*
Face: This is an unauthorized reception. You will be arrested and placed in detention for investigation. *The voice boldly and flatly states.*
Lilith: But . . . I was looking for Cecil. Where is Cecil. I'm his sister. I'm Elaine. I'm Elaine Harmsay. I'm just Cecil's sister. Isn't this the sanitation elimination room?
Face: We, we'll see about that shortly. Interceptors will be there immediately. Stay where you are. That is an order. *Voice trails off.*
Lilith: (Stutters) C. .can't. Got to find my brother or whatever. *Turns around and flees the intersection room.*

Suddenly, a large face of an Encoric Corporation bureaucrat loom large over Lilith; demanding that she be accountable for her unauthorized use of the spacial scan.

VERBAL DESCRIPTION

Starts with a man and woman exchanging harsh words at each other. It gets more and more heated as time goes on. You realize it is a husband and wife having a quarrel. This progresses into a very direct visual and verbal confrontation. Suddenly there is surprise and shock on both of their faces. The words stop and you gradually see the cause for the shock—a small boy looking up at them. Then the words with the parents looking down and child looking up.
Be careful, parents...someone is watching.

VISUAL DISCRIPTION

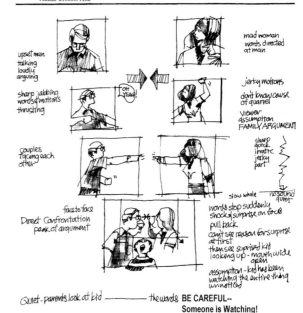

Dump Sheet

Increase Your Solutions and Ideas

It can be a real surprise when we find out the large amounts of information we know on any subject. We go through life collecting data, a fact here, a piece of information there. It all adds up to gobs of knowledge on all sorts of subjects. I've heard it said that the average person gets hit with about 3,000 facts each day. The problem is we usually haven't the foggiest idea of what we have collected over the years. Information is getting poured in all the time, but getting this information back out is sometimes impossible.

A simple tool called a *Dump Sheet* can help retrieve this information. A Dump Sheet is a large sheet of paper on which is listed all you know about a particular topic. There is no order to it, just a random list of all you can think about on a predetermined subject. These sheets can yank out of the dark corners of the mind previously lost data. Dump Sheets are very successful at collecting ideas. They serve as a tool for visually brainstorming, all the while providing an ever expanding visual record of the gathered ideas. →

Don't expect it to look pretty. Just list everything you can think of that relates to the problem you are considering.

Dump out all the ideas, facts, and related material you can think of on the problem or project at hand. It will surprise you what you know when it is on a sheet of paper in front of you. What follows are a seven points about this tool that may help.

A single sheet of paper

1 *Make sure that you use a big sheet of paper. People always put down more than they think they know about the problem.*

Don't use this size.   The bigger the better.

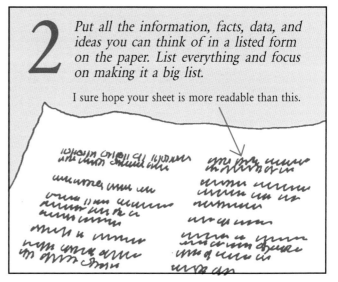

2 *Put all the information, facts, data, and ideas you can think of in a listed form on the paper. List everything and focus on making it a big list.*

I sure hope your sheet is more readable than this.

3 Avoid judging what is good or bad at this stage. Just list all the ideas you can think of.

4 After you have listed everything you can think of and this may take days, sit on it.

You may want to actually sit on it or do whatever it takes to get your mind away from the dump sheet and do other things.

5 When you come back to your list, review it and underline or make bold the key word for each point listed. This greatly helps in reading and reviewing the list later on.

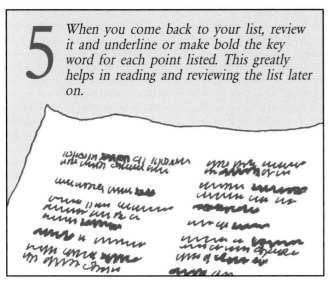

6 Rate each idea or point listed on the sheet with the following rating system.

Cross out for a bad or useless point.

Plus sign for a good point.

Bullet for just a point.

And the star for a really important point.

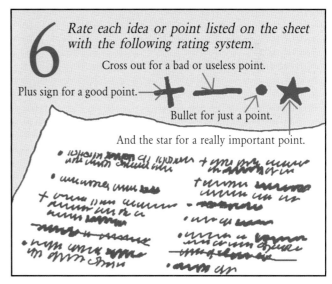

7 A Dump Sheet is a great visual device for finding out what you know and don't know about any particular problem or concern.

Use it alone or in a group setting. It is a great way to get others involved and build consensus.

Some people won't be of much help no matter what you use.

NOTE: Having the dump sheet pinned on the wall for all involved to see and add something helps increase the size of the list.

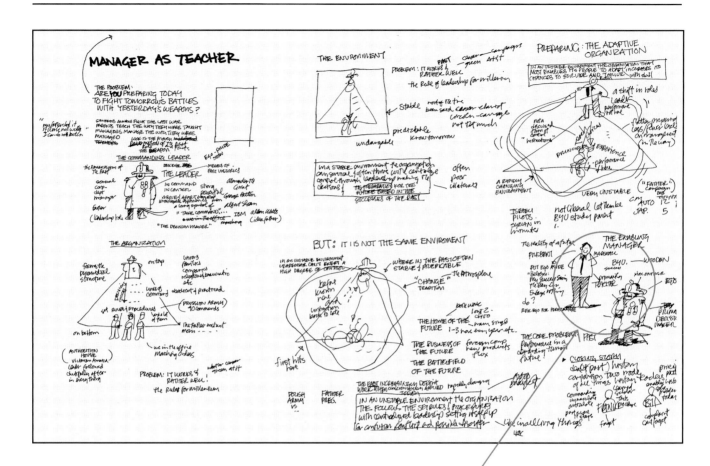

Two Kinds of Idea Collectors

There are basically two kinds of Dump Sheets. One is to have the group that is involved write down on a large sheet of paper any idea, concept, or information that they can think of that relates to the project or problem at hand. This is not done only at one sitting, such as a meeting, but works best by snagging those great ideas, over time, pasted on a wall or laid across a table. As contributing people walk by the Dump Sheet, it triggers their brain into contributing ideas to the sheet. It becomes a central collection point to grab everybody's mental contribution over at preset period of time, often taking days or even weeks to finally have enough ideas to actively work on.

The other kind of Dump Sheet serves as a visual collector. This one is done alone, or within a very limited group of designers and visualizers. Unlike the previous approach, this is usually done in one sitting. A person or small group draws random images on a sheet that are centered on resolving a problem or fleshing

This is a dump sheet for a chapter in a book. I didn't have the foggiest idea when I began that this is what I would end up with. The ideas and their connection to each other on the sheet took on a life all their own, dictating how the chapter would then develop.

out a concept. Each image builds on another until the large sheet is full of images, then moving on to filling up another sheet, if needed. Each sheet is sometimes hung on the wall until the entire room is covered up with these image-filled sheets.

In everyone's life there are those times when the mind

Here is a dump sheet on character development for a theme park project. The arrows indicate where I cut out each drawing then enlarged and pasted on individual sheets. Each character idea needed to be placed onto a single sheet for a developing concept presentation meeting.

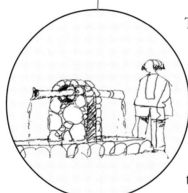

Then paste clippings from magazines, ripped out drawings from a note pad, and scribbled words on sticky notes. Make sure nothing you put onto the sheet is permanent. Remember everything temporary and removable. No pressure—just whenever you have anything that relates, or even may relate, stick it on the paper. Feel free to move things around or remove them.

Ideas will start to grow on the paper like little plants or spots of mold. With a Dump Sheet, what was work before is now just a little effort on the side. But this sideline dabbling produces more results than could all that previous hard effort.

I've just told you how this book began.

is blank—totally blank. There is nothing but air inside the skull and it's stale air. You end up going in circles, producing zero, repeatedly traveling back to where you started. For times like these, try using a Dump Sheet.

Removed from the daily traffic of people and conversation, put up on a wall a large sheet of blank paper.

Powerful Ideas Simply Portrayed

To effectively compete in today's world we must have the right information. In the information age, we depend more and more on having the knowledge we need to effectively do our job. But accessing that knowledge through a growing overload of facts, data, figures, and concepts is getting harder to do. We waste precious time going through piles of data to find what is relevant. We need a more effective way to accomplish this increasingly more difficult job.

To deal with all this growing overload of information, I invented a visual communication device called *Quickscans.* These are visual summaries of relevant information that are easily read and applied. They are learning tools to more effectively and more quickly provide important, relevant knowledge. Quickscans are simple and entertaining pages or screens that are used to teach complex ideas in minutes.

The pages are first made with an underlying diagram or schematic that visually and symbolically represents the information or knowledge to be communicated. This diagram's or schematic's purpose is to capture the essential meaning and content of what is being communicated in as simple a visual structure as possible. Doing this takes a good deal of time and effort to develop this underlying visual. Making it simple isn't always easy, but when this essential visual is finally completed, everything else is built over it. →

Here are three Quickscans I've used in the past. The top one contains a content summary for an exhibit, next is a visual summary of a best-selling book, and finally the bottom one was used in a presentation.

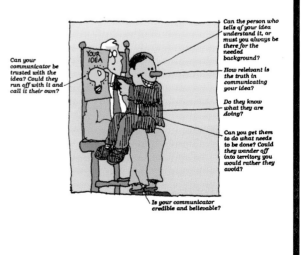

Break Down

THE 3 BIGGEST PROBLEMS CAUSING COMPUTER BREAKDOWN

Even the gem of our technological revolution isn't exempt from the effects of Murphy's Law. I'm sorry to let this out, but computers do break down. They are not the perfect machines we are led to believe.

Computer breakdown can be separated into these areas:

> "The majority of problems we usually have are the obvious things, such as plugging in the computer and loading the software."
>
> Fred Yates
> Owner of a computer store

1 The **PEOPLE** operating the equipment can make mistakes in setup and operation.

2 The **SOFTWARE** may contain errors in programming, causing faulty instruction to the computer.

3 The **COMPUTER** sometimes has hardware installed that is defective which causes poor functioning or it doesn't work at all.

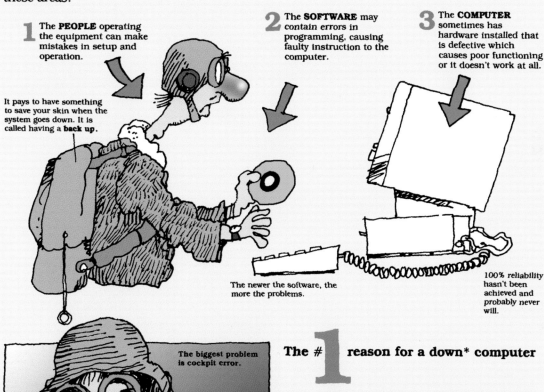

It pays to have something to save your skin when the system goes down. It is called having a **back up**.

The newer the software, the more the problems.

100% reliability hasn't been achieved and probably never will.

The biggest problem is cockpit error.

The #**1** reason for a down* computer

Most airplane accidents are the fault of pilot error. The one in the electronic cockpit causes the majority of computer errors also. **Most problems originate in the brain behind the brain.**

The Key Solution

The solution is in knowledge and experience. The more you know, the fewer problems you will have. This applies to flying machines of any kind.

Crash a sudden failure of a computer system.
Down Time The time a computer is down and not working.

* When a computer is down, it is a polite way of saying the blasted machine is busted.

NOTE: The Quickscan above was first presented in a talk I had to give and later used in a computer book. This simple concept was more memorable by making it into a single page Quickscan.

An industrial design single-view Quickscan used in teaching a college course.

CONVOLUTION

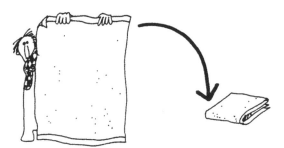

BASIC CONCEPT: To obtain the maximum surface area or exposure in the minimum amount of space, fold, or convolute the surface.

Example: In order to store a large blanket under the bed, you must fold it. The large surface of the blanket is convoluted or folded into the smallest area.

Other examples of convolution:

At the back of some electronic equipment, there is a slotted piece of metal called a heat sink. This protective device dissipates heat by exposing a large surface area to the cooler air in the least space.

The intestines are convoluted to have the maximum surface contact with the food to extract the most nutrients in the least space.

Curtains must cover the entire window when the window is closed, but fold to the side when the window is opened.

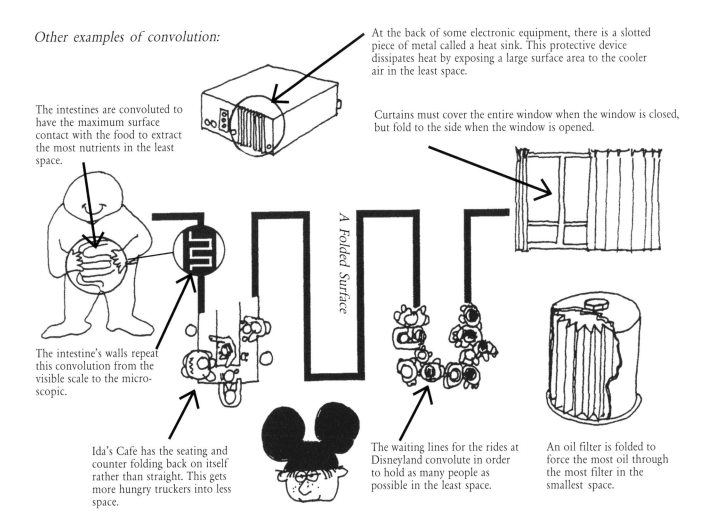

A Folded Surface

The intestine's walls repeat this convolution from the visible scale to the microscopic.

Ida's Cafe has the seating and counter folding back on itself rather than straight. This gets more hungry truckers into less space.

The waiting lines for the rides at Disneyland convolute in order to hold as many people as possible in the least space.

An oil filter is folded to force the most oil through the most filter in the smallest space.

NOTE: When put into such a simple and entertaining format as a Quickscan, any information that you need to communicate will have an improved chance at being accepted, understood, and applied.

Images that entertain and inform are then drawn over this visual foundation. Copy is added for explanation and clarity. Stories and relevant facts are added to link this repackaged information to the viewer's own life.

Quickscans are usually handed out after some kind of presentation, communicating the information contained in its pages. They serve as a memory device to retain the presented information or knowledge. The important measure of any Quickscan's success is found in how much information is retained and applied after reviewing it.

These finished Quickscans seem to have a unique life all their own. They remain in full view taped on cubicle walls or pasted into new reports, long after their intended life span; and are resurrected each time modified into communicating some new and different information.

More Quickscans communicating a wide range information in a variety of situations.

SPECIAL NOTE: A secret to getting a Quickscan to work is to get all the important information boiled down to a single diagram or chart, then repackaging it into a simple and entertaining format.

Vehicles For Delivering Creative Ideas

You can't understand a new idea without linking it in some way to what you already know. The usual link for what is known to what is unknown is a metaphor. A metaphor is an idea or concept understood in one area that is similar to the properties or process in another new area.

A metaphor is the world of 'is like.' This is like that. A metaphor compares the meaning and attributes of one thing to the meaning and attributes of something else. A viral infection is like the spread of an idea. A company's future direction is a long and interesting journey into unknown territory. She comes and goes like the wind. You can't offend him, he's really thick-skinned.

In the rapid visualization of ideas, metaphors are a common device to visually wrap new ideas inside. Something known and understood by the visualizer is the vehicle used to deliver a new and original idea, helping to illustrate and expand the needed understanding.

The images used in the rapid visualization of ideas for various projects, concepts, proposals, and presentations may be insufficient. The ideas may need an added metaphoric dimension to be understood. A picture with a rectangle and some notes may be insufficient. The shape should be roots carrying nutrients up into a tree. The image of circle with a title written inside it may just not pull off what you want. The circle may need to be the sun with the nine planets revolving around it. An interior sketch may need to be packaged inside the metaphor of a seed germinating to be appreciated. Images carry a deeper meaning and understanding when they are metaphorical. Here are the most common areas for metaphors that you can draw for more profound understanding and insight.

1 Activities Constructing a table, baking a cake, playing a board game, eating an apple, taking a shower, leading an orchestra, painting a landscape, writing a letter, weeding a garden, watching television, giving a lecture, reading a book, making love, moving, and buying a car.

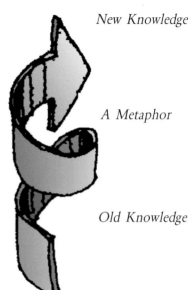

Learning by metaphor works in a spiral. Start with a base of knowledge then move up through the metaphor by comparing what is known to the unknown. The result is new knowledge, which in turn becomes old knowledge, to again repeat this same metaphorical learning process.

New Knowledge

A Metaphor

Old Knowledge

All sorts of the activities of life are possible, with the more commonly known, being the best to use when communicating with groups.

2 Buildings Houses, stores, office buildings, rooms, tents, motor homes, huts, and the parts of buildings, such as facades, foyers, rest rooms, and living rooms can a serve as a metaphor for the packaging of an idea. Because they are where we spend so much time they easily serve as a solid ground to make a creative jump into something new.

Putting your images into the metaphor of a building can be a new added dimension to your ideas.

3 Living Things Flora, fauna, bugs, frogs, roses, whales, daisies, ants, flies, taxi cab drivers, groupers, geese, dandelions, bread mold, pelicans, and giraffes can represent something new.

Making something we see and know helps us understand what we don't see and can't comprehend. This makes the living thing and the concept being communicated both come alive.

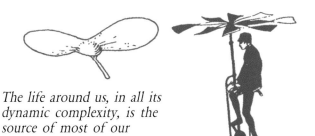

The life around us, in all its dynamic complexity, is the source of most of our understanding.

4 Stages Production stages, growth stages, stages of conception, stages of a missile, stages of acceptance, stages of product development, stages of building, and stages of just about anything can help provide the source for images and metaphors of those ideas you are trying to create and communicate.

5 Machines Motors, corkscrews, engines, CD players, cameras, computers, kidney machines, drills, pipe extruders, saws, and asphalt layers are machines to allow deeper understanding into a proposed idea.

Devices made to expand our abilities can be metaphorically used to expand our minds. A diagram is just that, but becomes more when it's an electrical circuit for a flashlight.

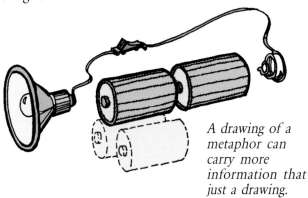

A drawing of a metaphor can carry more information that just a drawing.

NOTE: I believe that all thinking is metaphorical. Everything inside our heads are representations of all the stuff in the outside world.

6 Systems Ecological, financial, digestive, social, ecumenical, circulatory, and solar systems are where the whole is greater than the sum of any of the parts. Systems are where complex ideas can be placed into an interrelated and cohesive structure for understanding and interaction. Complexity can be made fully comprehensible using a system's metaphor.

7 Vehicles Ships, planes, cars, sleighs, skate boards, spaceships, elevators, roller skates, and submarines can let a drawing of one thing represent the ideas and concepts of another. A vehicle metaphor can very effectively carry an idea to where you want it to go.

8 Journeys Marco Polo, Columbus, Ulysses, mystical, historical, personal, nomadic, point A to point B, and side trips can all help move your audience into new terrain a lot easier, allowing everyone involved, even the visualizer, into an interesting trip.

9 Landscapes Ocean, jungle, reef, rain forest, savanna, prairie, mountain, desert, city, suburbia, airport, and corner store can all serve as landscapes for insights.

RULE 503: If it's a business meeting in Texas always use a football metaphor to get your ideas across.

10 Events Games, historical events, hysterical events, parties, elections, battles, and coronations are situations and contexts you can use to illustrate a point, win a contract, or carry on a project.

Generate Better Creative Ideas Easier

Brainstorming is one of the most effective techniques for coming up with new ideas. In this technique, a selected group of people put aside their judgements and concentrate on the goal of coming up with as many new ideas as possible. In the allotted time they collectively try for the maximum number of solutions, using one idea to trigger another, pulling a concept out of the air, and involving everybody in the act of listing anything and everything that even absurdly could resolve the given problem. Idea volume is the key, putting off the job of idea selection and evaluation until much later.

Now put this idea generating process into a collection of visual images and you're using *Graphic Ideation*. Have everyone involved in idea generation visually record their ideas, just a note and some image to describe the idea then quickly moving on, but having just one person visually record the group's contribution on large sheets or rolls of paper is a more common approach. Seeing the process of everyone's contribution creates a consensus and focus that is both very creative and productive.

Visually recording ideas as they tumble out of contributing minds can add a depth and richness to any brainstorming session.

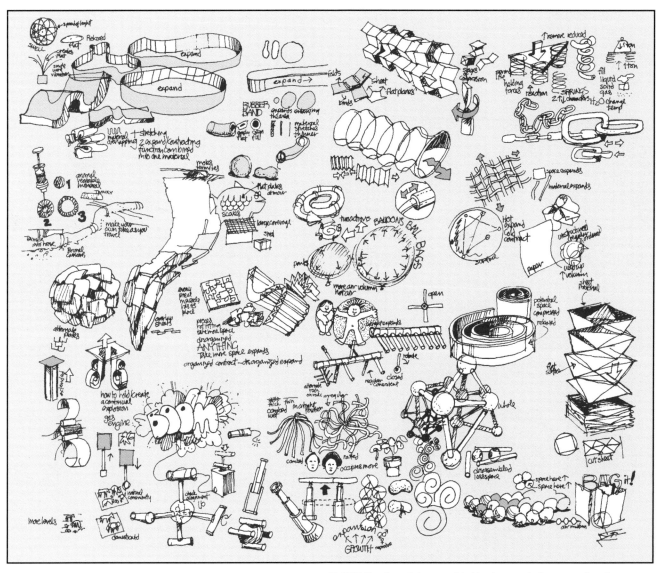

NOTE: I've found that graphic ideation works best on rolls of paper, not sheets. Rolls of butcher paper or the end-rolls from the web presses of printers are my usual sources of my ideation paper.

Often the sheets from a graphic ideation session aren't very readable. Only the people involved could tell you what the scribbled images mean. *As long as it works for the situation, that's fine.*

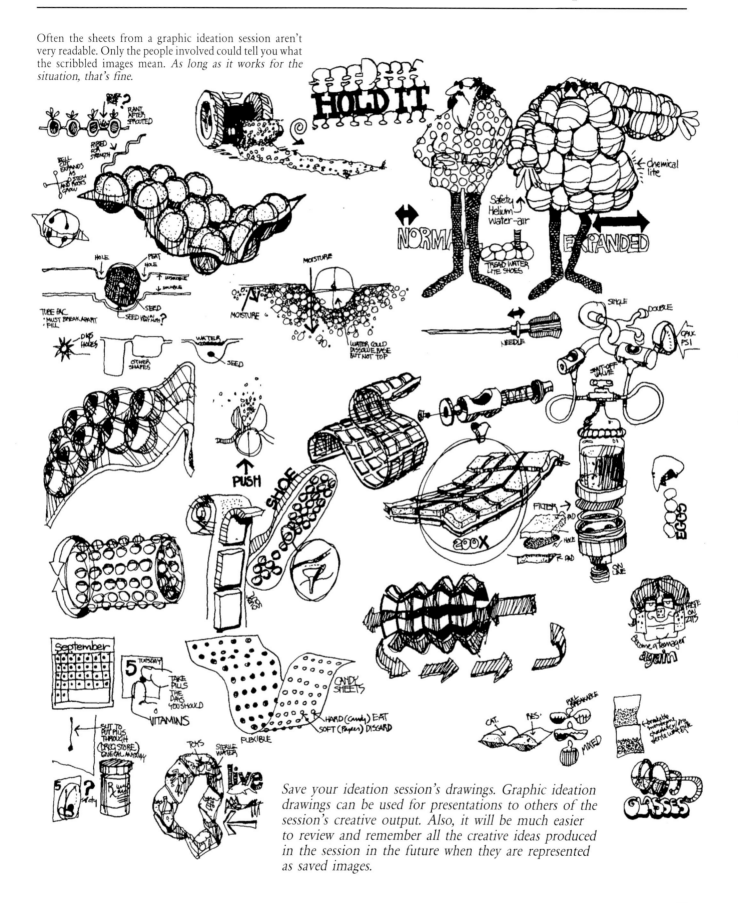

Save your ideation session's drawings. Graphic ideation drawings can be used for presentations to others of the session's creative output. Also, it will be much easier to review and remember all the creative ideas produced in the session in the future when they are represented as saved images.

Capture The Ideas Most People Miss

In order to remember and utilize those ideas that come to me in various ways on a daily basis, I put them on little note cards. What began years ago as a simple notation tool has now resulted in thousands of these cards. Each card contains one idea with a few notes and a quickly drawn image.

There are always a few of these cards in my shirt pocket, by the bed on the night stand, and even some emergency cards stuffed in my wallet. I never know when an idea or concept will hit me and it needs to be captured. So far these powerful little cards have resulted in over 20 books, numerous presentations, design solutions, and management concepts and insights that I wouldn't have gained in any other way. *Capture Cards* are an effective and easy tool to use, even when semidiligently applied, like I do.

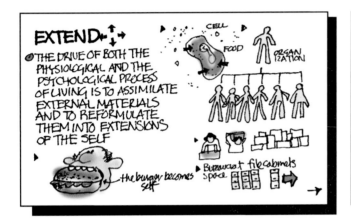

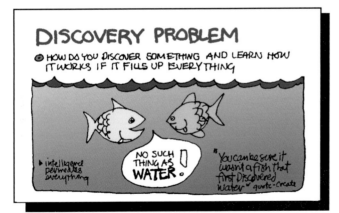

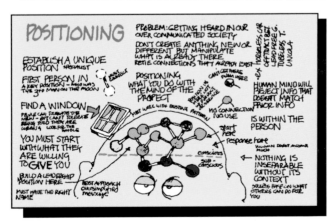

NOTE: These cards can save you time in presenting concepts to groups by enlarging them to eight times their size for wall mounted presentations.

I usually put the title of the cards in bold and/or in larger lettering in the upper left hand side this helps in later locating this card.

The cards I used in the past were 3X 5 now they are 4 X 6 blank cards. I need these cards larger now to see them more clearly (This will happen to you, too).

The central or core image is often all that is needed to recall the concept or idea when accessing the card in the future.

Each Capture Card has a central visual or image illustrating the concept or idea captured by the card.

Toll Position

a position in which people must pay for each use.

only way

- bridge analogy
- a tempory situation
- must work without effort after the initial set up

- process product service etc
- power position
- best source for service product or combination

over

I've tried all sorts of ways to collect these cards into some kind of accessing system (I have even used a computer program).

But what works the best is the easiest, just a card file. The cards are filed randomly, facilitating those lucky accidents caused from juxtaposed ideas.

↗Here is an example of a Capture Card and the finished pages in a book resulting from the idea visualized on that card.

A little note or arrow on the bottom says there is more on the other side of the card.

Toll Position— Keep the Money Coming

Get yourself in a key position where you can charge a toll.

Make sure it is as easy as possible for someone to utilize your idea.

Charge a toll that is reasonable to the user.

25¢ Toll Booth

Encourage any outside inducements to use your idea.

Maintain the key elements.

A satisfied user is one who returns.

TOLL POSITION—KEEP THE MONEY COMING

Paul Anka wrote the Tonight Show theme many years ago—and charged a toll. He gets $30,000 a year from it, every year.

Keep a wary eye on any and all competition.

You're driving down a new road. Nice and easy. Then you see a row of booths across the road. Oh-oh. You have to stop and pay a toll to use the road. You dig deep and pull out your quarter. You're not sure you want to pay, but that's the only way they'll let you drive on the road. So probably it's worth it.

The city planners put up a bridge. They don't want to charge all the taxpayers—just those who use the bridge. How do they do it? They charge a toll. You dig deep for another quarter.

Tolls are great inventions. They're so great that everyone should try to get a toll bridge or road all his own.

That's what innovators should do. Get in a toll position. Then every time people use the creation the creator gets paid.

How can you charge a toll? Some examples:

- **royalties** if you're an author, you get paid a percentage on every book of yours that's sold. If you're a songwriter, you get a percentage on every copy of your song that sells. If you own mineral rich land, you get a percentage of every ton of coal they pull out of your land.

- **usage fees** lend some money and you get to charge a percentage every month. Let someone

rent your apartment and you get a payment every month.

- **appreciation** as time passes, your land or gold grows more valuable; you can charge more for it.

Collecting Payment for Your Idea

Rather than sell your idea outright, get in a toll position. Then you can get regular payments for it, just as if you were collecting a quarter for every car that drives on a toll road. Here's how:

1. **Set it up** so it will work without effort. Have the people pay for usage. Have a royalty contract, usage fee, rental agreement, license requirement, subscription arrangement.

2. **Charge your toll** for products, services, or a combination of both.

3. **Maintain a power position,** so you'll be able to control the toll.

4. **Remember that tolls are always only temporary**—a new road is built, people start to take an alternate route, someone puts up a free bridge next to your toll bridge. Your toll can't last forever, but until it ends, use it for all it's worth.

If you charge a toll every time someone uses your idea, you'll make a lot more money.

56

57

The word CHARRETTE was originally derived from the French name for the CART a master artist would use to collect the daily work of their apprentice students.

What Is A Charrette?

A *Charrette* is a team-based, idea-formulating technique for developing and planning a project. It involves bringing together a group of experienced professionals from different disciplines into a session to jointly concentrate on, stimulate, and formulate workable ideas and to develop the guiding criteria for a project's further development. A Charrette is a group management tool and the first step in a long process that is designed to quickly establish a project's concept, vision, and governing criteria. A Charrette is not just a brainstorming session. It is a carefully orchestrated event where the participants, schedule, and location are chosen to encourage a focused creativity within a structured framework.

What Is A Charrette Good For?

A Charrette concentrates on pulling together the right people with the necessary skills to make a decision within a relatively short period of time, saving substantial time and money. The final result of a Charrette is a concrete plan which allows key decision makers to visualize and understand the practical implications of a project's concept. It helps them catch an over-arching vision of the project outcome and the critical steps needed to achieve that vision. It identifies fatal flaws, improving the effectiveness of the key decisions about its viability or concept before investing, answering the key questions of "What is this project?" and "Is it worthwhile?"

How Do You Create a Charrette?

Here are the steps necessary to creating and running an effective and successful Charrette:

1 Setting Up The Charrette The critical factor at any Charrette's beginning is the selection of a facilitator to manage the Charrette session. A facilitator isn't required to have any specific background but must have an overall understanding of the Charrette process. This means a facilitator must be able to: 1) lead the group in finding their way in uncharted territory; 2) recognize what constitutes progress; 3) balance careful analysis with flash-of-insight creativity. The facilitator is responsible for setting the pace of the meeting, acting as moderator, analyst, or creator to ensure that time limits are adhered to and channel everyone's contributions into productive results.

The facilitator selects and prepares the right number and types of people to participate in the Charrette, then establishes the optimal time and place of the Charrette with the purpose and desired outcome clear to all invited. Picking the right people, 8 to 12 in number, will help to ensure a Charrette's success. They should have divergent areas of experience and expertise and are usually from such areas as feasibility analysis, design, operations, etc. Make sure they cover the needed expertise demanded by the project. Avoid people with an ax to grind and inflexibility. They must be willing to sometimes lead and sometimes follow. They must be willing to contribute their best thoughts to the group's efforts without care for defending their ego. It will then be the facilitator's job to forge these selected people into a temporary workable team.

The session's defining criteria needs to be established and sent beforehand, coupled with a packet of helpful information, to all the people attending the session. This packet lets everyone know what to expect with a clear and easy-to-read agenda (with time allocations), background materials on similar, comparable, or competing projects, and basic contextual facts surrounding the project. The materials should help a prepared attendee to see important patterns, concept approaches, or idea relationships. This session's defining criteria is only a few pages long, with other support materials taking less than an hour or so to read. Conciseness, clarity, and brevity are at a premium here. Participants don't need to be overloaded, just prepared.

Having a successful charrette involves the completion of the following five steps:

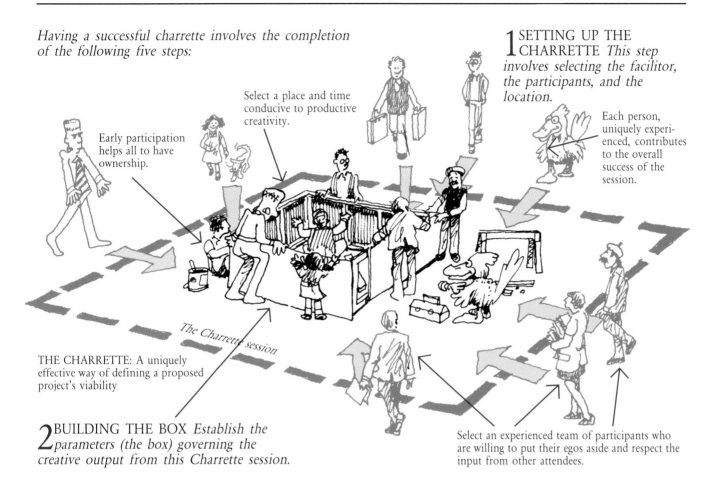

1 SETTING UP THE CHARRETTE *This step involves selecting the facilitor, the participants, and the location.*

Select a place and time conducive to productive creativity.

Each person, uniquely experienced, contributes to the overall success of the session.

Early participation helps all to have ownership.

The Charrette session

THE CHARRETTE: A uniquely effective way of defining a proposed project's viability

2 BUILDING THE BOX *Establish the parameters (the box) governing the creative output from this Charrette session.*

Select an experienced team of participants who are willing to put their egos aside and respect the input from other attendees.

Finally, you must select a place conducive to the sometimes-opposing demands of both creativity and productivity that will hopefully occur in the Charrette. Holding the session at work always allows for the imposition of outside demands, interrupting the group's chain of thought.

Also allow enough wall space to paste all the team's thoughts. This space must be visible to everyone in the room with its collection of various sheets of paper showing in words, pictures, and diagrams where everyone is at any given moment. These visuals help to concentrate the group's attention and facilitate relational thinking. A nice environment with big open walls and away from the interrupting demands of work typically functions best.

An important point: *The more you have the right people working in the right place in the right way focusing on the right problem, the more effective your Charrette will become.*

2 **Building The Box** Much is written about *"thinking outside the box."* To achieve the Charrette's goals thinking is *"inside the box,"* but it's a new box. Parameters must be placed on all participants and on the project itself, like that of "a box" to hold their ideas and set the governing criteria for the project. Without a box, a Charrette is just another idea session. Building a box, within which all the ideas generated must fit, requires an understanding of rigid and flexible box criteria and the size and type of ideas to be placed. This involves physical, emotional, financial, scheduling, and even political constraints.

Creating a box means creating boundaries that describe what factors about a proposed idea or concept will and won't work.

This is not an easy task, but requires a kind of nonjudgmental decision. Remember, the clearer the constraints *(the box)*, the more powerful the →

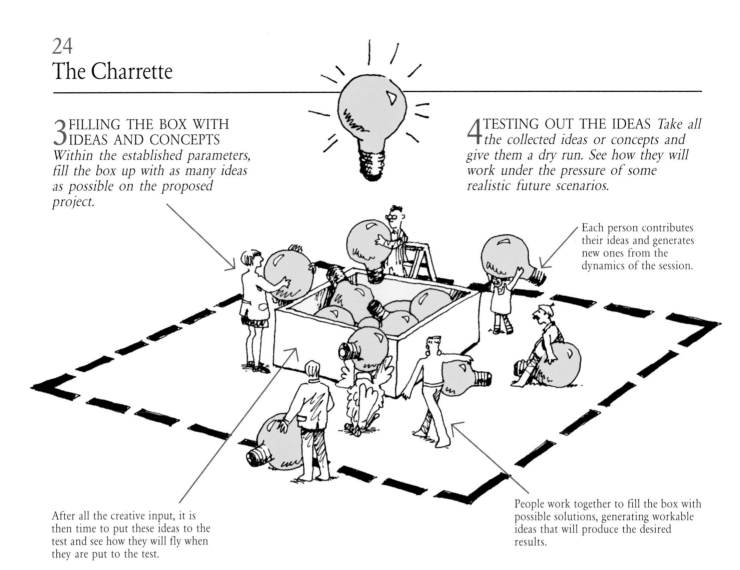

3 FILLING THE BOX WITH IDEAS AND CONCEPTS
Within the established parameters, fill the box up with as many ideas as possible on the proposed project.

4 TESTING OUT THE IDEAS *Take all the collected ideas or concepts and give them a dry run. See how they will work under the pressure of some realistic future scenarios.*

Each person contributes their ideas and generates new ones from the dynamics of the session.

After all the creative input, it is then time to put these ideas to the test and see how they will fly when they are put to the test.

People work together to fill the box with possible solutions, generating workable ideas that will produce the desired results.

final concept will be. A box that will not hold new ideas will just recreate old problems.

Typical thinking says "Allowing more time will generate more ideas," but setting an optimal time frame will actually achieve optimal results. Since a Charrette is limited by time for idea generation and analysis, it is critical to place the right amount of pressure on participants to stimulate thought and ideas. Plus, setting game rules early gets everyone involved and establishes a sense of joint ownership. Any successful Charrette has the single strong expectation of "taking apart a project" then reassembling it into "something more."

3 **Filling The Box With Ideas** Creativity is typically thought of as the generation of wacky and off-the-wall ideas, but within a Charrette this creativity is bound within the economic, social, political, etc. constraints dictated by the project. The fun of idea generation is channeled by a need for practical results. The group dynamics should focus on fitting the ideas

into the defining boundaries that have been established. If the box doesn't seem to work, place it on the shelf temporarily and build a new box, adjusting and combining both as the work progresses. Combining both creative and analytical thinking polarizes a bad team into becoming stuck, but it unifies a good team into producing a successful solution. The utilization of idea generation techniques is initiated, but in a Charrette the ideas generated tend to be in a set direction. Within these limits, idea volume and quality are the driving forces. More is better and nutty, crazy ideas are just fine. Then, judge not, because evaluation of these ideas is always separate and placed in the next step.

The dialogue during this stage is very open, with people constantly suggesting ideas, and without limitations on who may comment when. Ideas put forward are born from both original thought and experience, but also collectively build and link with the groups' combined wisdom and skill.

In addition, this kind of creativity requires conceptual thinking, visual images, and the ability to be inspired by the ideas given by other members of the session. During the Charrette, the members skilled in rapid visualization provide and collect verbal ideas from all the participants and create quickly sketched visual images to convey these concepts. These visual descriptions of ideas unite the group around the image and ideas they communicate in a way that using only verbal or word concepts cannot.

4 Testing Out The Ideas There is another level of analytical creativity that requires the pro-cess of successful working within a framework, while beating up the ideas to prove their performance. Creativity is seldom thought of as ideas generated in a targeted direction and limited by time and output. See if these ideas fly and check out how they will do in the real world by looking into the project's future. Walk through and test out every idea to some degree.

In a successful Charrette, the attendees in an atmosphere of productive fun and with a respect for the expertise of others, participate in this process to produce outstanding results that can only be termed as truly magical.

Sometimes a person needs to be selected to present the final concept to the project's sponsors.

5 SELECTING THE BEST CONCEPT
One concept or idea is selected by the joint involvement and analysis of the group. Pick that one concept that will work best at defining and directing the project's future development.

5 Selecting The Best Concept This stage picks the best concept to optimally produce the desired results within the constraints of the project, looking for the one concept that will insure the best investment in the project's final success. Sometimes it is best to lay your top ideas out in front of everyone. This allows a better comparison between each idea and makes the input from everyone involved much easier. Restate to everyone the purpose and defining constraints for the Charrette, then collectively struggle for a consensus in selecting that one best idea. This stage is when the reason for the Charrette comes to fruition, the time when everyone is tired but their joint success can be measured by their productive results.

A Charrette Is A Powerful Tool To Use When Beginning A Project

A successful Charrette is a small price to pay in the beginning of a project's development and will save huge amounts of investment in money, time, and resources. Instead of hurriedly rushing a project towards its final creation, stopping the project's momentum for a short time and having a Charrette can provide a major boost towards making the entire project realistically work and work well.

Hands-On Knowledge

Overcoming Creative Block

I've found that when I'm stuck and can't come up with any new ideas or can't get the drawings to really work it is usually the result of being *too distant* from the context I'm trying to design and draw for.

I remember a project where I was directing a team of designers and we were all stuck. No matter how many tricks I tried and how many days we spent pounding our heads, we stayed stuck—no ideas, no drawings. The ideas only started to flow when all of us drove to a store and got physically involved. At that store was the actual product and real customers that we were trying to abstractly design for from miles away. Walking around the store we suddenly came up with all sorts of great ideas more than we could possibly handle. We had been too physically distant from the world we were trying to design.

I call it getting *Hands-On* knowledge. As the physical distance increases, the conceptual/thinking and drawing/visualizing distance also increases. There is a direct link between touching, smelling, tasting, and actually seeing something and our creative minds. Plus, using computers and other technology often only increases this distance. Sometimes we are mentally stuck because we're just too distant, too physically separate, from what we are trying to design and draw.

Getting your hands on it, into it, and all over it creates a dynamic creative process that can not be achieved in any other way. Whenever you're stuck with a blank sheet of paper that stays blank try getting your hands on something you can physically feel.

Here are three Hands-On techniques that I often use when visualizing. The one below I actually used on the two pages you're looking at.

1 *I was stuck on how to create this unit. It remained staring at me as blank paper until I actually drew the pages as a thumbnail.*

Then I enlarged this thumbnail to the size of the final pages would actually be. I even placed the enlarged copies into a book I had laying around that was the same size as this book was going to be.

Then something odd happened with this Hands-On technique. I actually started to read the line-indicated copy.

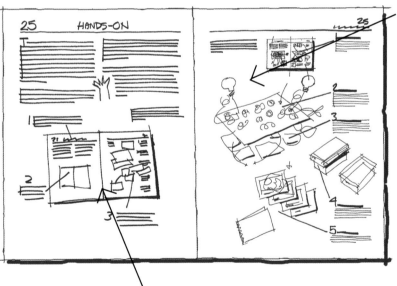

Thumbnails work great at showing concepts without allowing those mind-boggling details.

Once this little drawing was enlarged into the actually sized pages and put into a book everything else fell into place.

NOTE: I couldn't tell you where the letters on a keyboard are to save me, but as soon as I begin to type, my hands know. I believe there is unique knowledge located only in our hands.

2 *Still another Hands-On technique is to do something totally different. Get your senses involved with something that isn't related to anything your are doing.*

I find doing something physically different with my hands that I don't have to think about actually shifts a stuck brain.

3 *This next Hands-On technique works extremely well. I visually dump everything I can think of or collect on a large sheet of paper. There is no order to where I put what, other than space.*

Then I physically cut the ideas I like out of this sheet and enlarge and paste them into a rough set of finished-sized drawings.

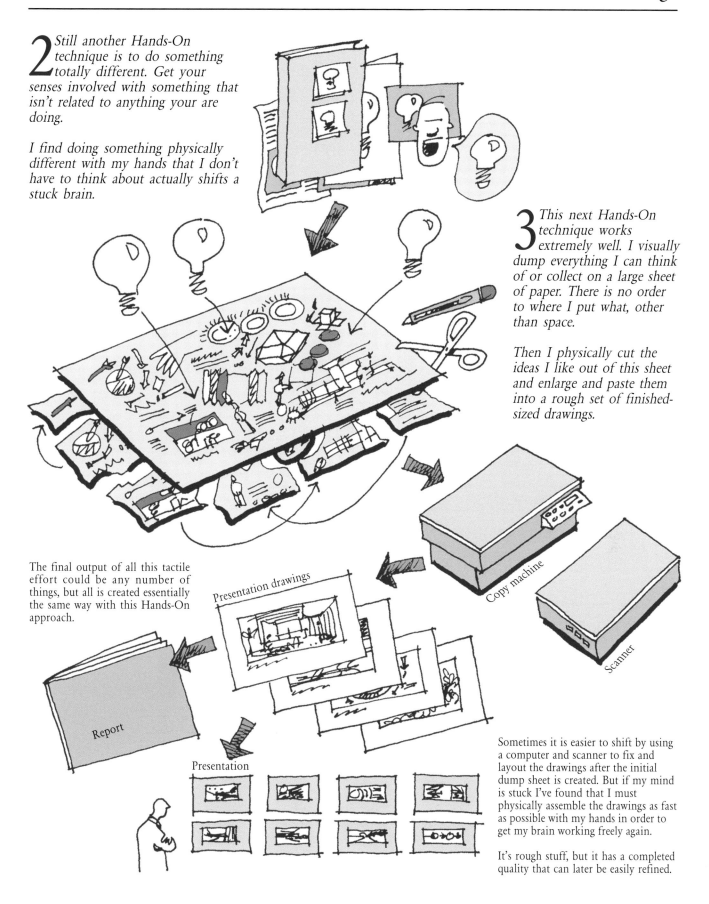

Copy machine

Scanner

The final output of all this tactile effort could be any number of things, but all is created essentially the same way with this Hands-On approach.

Presentation drawings

Report

Presentation

Sometimes it is easier to shift by using a computer and scanner to fix and layout the drawings after the initial dump sheet is created. But if my mind is stuck I've found that I must physically assemble the drawings as fast as possible with my hands in order to get my brain working freely again.

It's rough stuff, but it has a completed quality that can later be easily refined.

A Creative Record Of Your Creativity

Because I have dyslexia, I've had to make visual notes all of my life. I found when I was in school, if I put an idea into some kind of visual image I could then better use and remember it. So my notes have always had visual elements to them.

Years later, when working as a designer I realized how truly effective visual notation can be with complex projects involving very diverse groups of people. People kept asking for copies of my notes and would refer to what was written and drawn on my notes throughout the early development sessions. These notes would →

→ *Visual notation and the finished photograph of a museum project showing how the ideas were carried to completion. It's surprising how closely they match.*

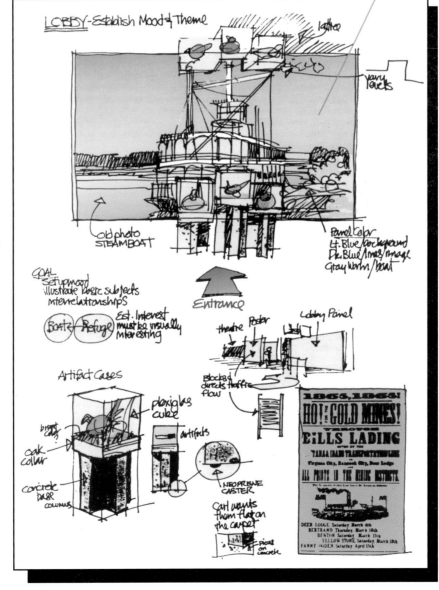

Visual notes for this museum project were quite extensive because of the diversity and complexity of information needing to be communicated to the visitor.

Visual notes help structure information, develop criteria and visualize possibilities.

→ *Visual notes from a project on character development. All of the sheets for this project were easy to scan and retrieve because of their visual format.*

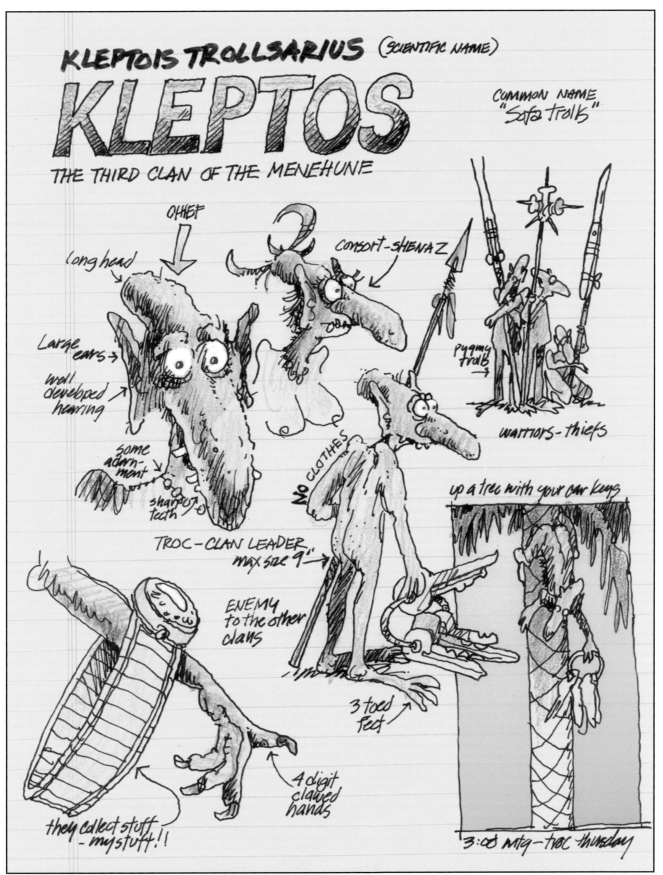

NOTE: Visual notes take more time at first than the usual word-only approach, but they can accomplish move and be used to save drawing time later on.

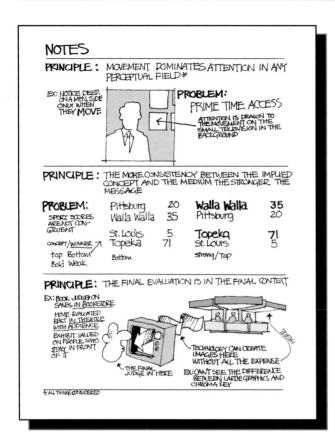

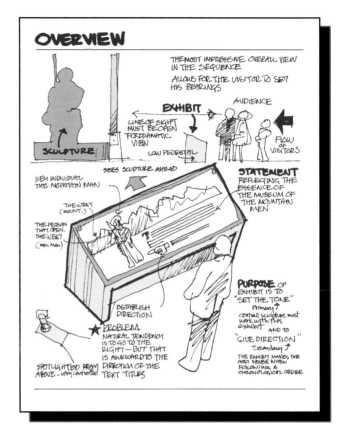

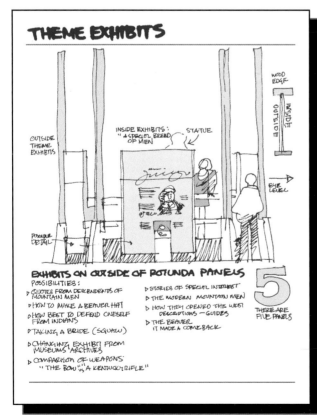

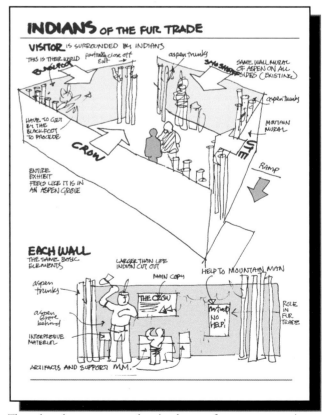

The top left page is a redesign for a news show on a TV station.

The other three pages are the visual notes for a musem project featuring history of the early American fur trade.

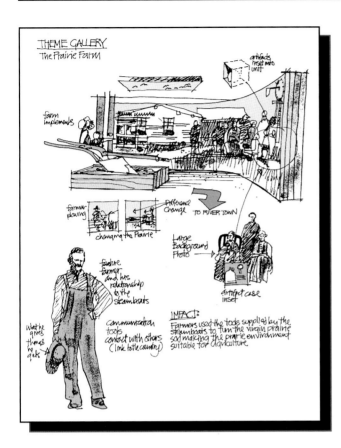

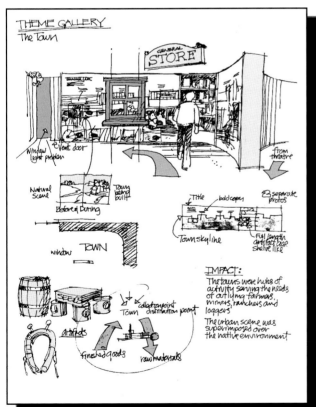

Above are visual notes from another historical museum, this one featuring a raised steam ship that had sunk in the late 1800s.

often set the direction and definition for an entire project.

It took me awhile to get use to this. In the past I would keep my odd way of note taking a secret and deliberately hide them by covering my notes with something or by turning the notes over to the blank other side. And rightly so. I particularly remember one scolding by an irate teacher who found my notes. They threw them in the trash and commanded, "That is no way to take proper notes. Leave your art drawings in the art class. Now go and do them right and I don't want to see one single picture."

Some people will never see the real value of visual note taking, but you wouldn't be one of them if you were reading this. If you aren't already doing it, change your written note taking into drawings with notation. Then try it and show them to others. Your visual note taking will take on a new clarity, creativity, and communicative power that the word-only notes don't have.

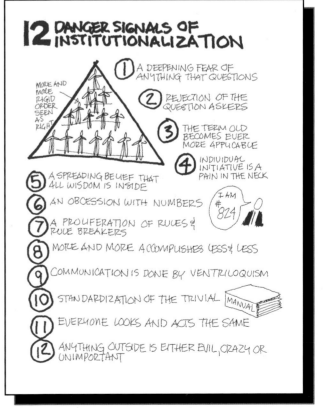

My notes for a book on motivating employees.

Drawing For A Competitive Edge

This is one of those drawing techniques that IS hard to explain, not because it's difficult, but because it's different. *Visualizing Tactics* often require drawing what is hidden. Most people or groups seldom look at their tactics or strategies. They just assume they're doing things the right way they are to be done.

When using Visualizing Tactics you function as an aside person, a facilitator, the man-from-Mars, whose sole purpose is to show with images, metaphors, and symbols how everyone is *thinking about what they are thinking of doing.* When you are in this role you are visually reflecting back to the people involved their underlying assumptions on how things will work—their tactics.

The best place to do this is in a small group or team that is flexible and willing to see things differently. The last thing an entrenched and rigid group wants to see is their tactics, their real tactics, in solving a problem or developing alternatives. Typically with large groups when you start visually reflecting back to them their diverse underlying tactics things can fall into real chaos fast. But with a small group of motivated individuals willing to really look at themselves, the process can be fun and very interesting.

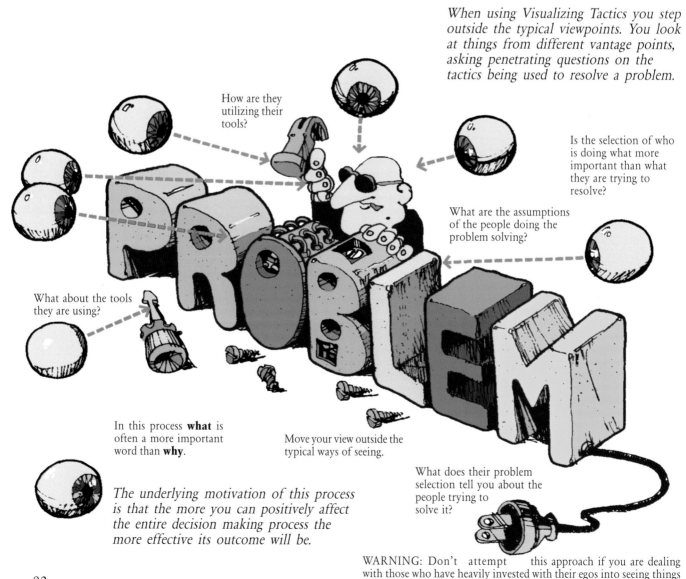

When using Visualizing Tactics you step outside the typical viewpoints. You look at things from different vantage points, asking penetrating questions on the tactics being used to resolve a problem.

How are they utilizing their tools?

Is the selection of who is doing what more important than what they are trying to resolve?

What are the assumptions of the people doing the problem solving?

What about the tools they are using?

In this process **what** is often a more important word than **why**.

Move your view outside the typical ways of seeing.

What does their problem selection tell you about the people trying to solve it?

The underlying motivation of this process is that the more you can positively affect the entire decision making process the more effective its outcome will be.

WARNING: Don't attempt this approach if you are dealing with those who have heavily invested with their egos into seeing things from a rigid and predetermined viewpoint. You'll suffer!

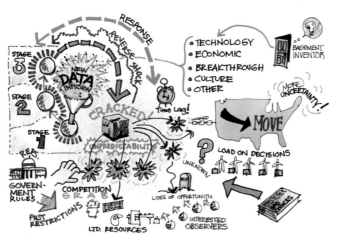

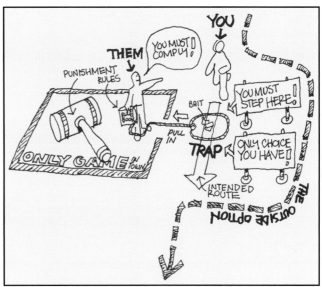

↑A tactical schematic done in front of a group. Doing this level of drawing in a group setting helps builds consensus.

↓This is the first time I've ever seen a drawing like this in a book. It is messy, it centers on reality, and it focuses on the real tactics, but it is dangerous if the wrong people see it.

↑This is a drawing for a manager to show her how she had other options than the ones she was being forced or tricked into accepting. She still talks about the importance of this simple visualization was to her.

The typical images or schematics of tactics are always presented as clean and precise drawings. But the reality of the real tactics that are actually used is always far different.

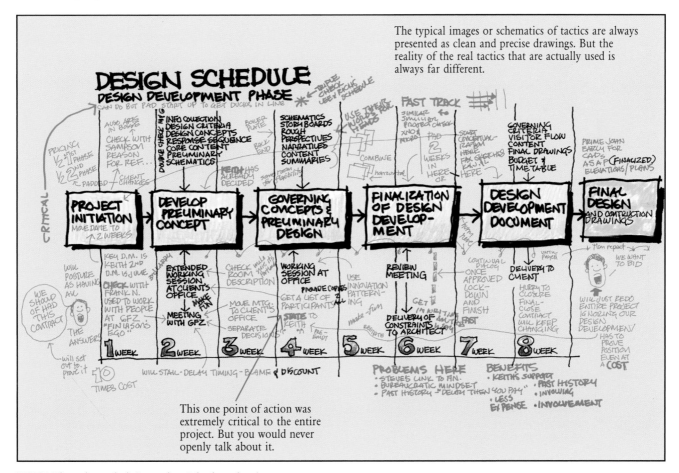

This one point of action was extremely critical to the entire project. But you would never openly talk about it.

NOTE: The only symbols I use when I do these drawings are common typical symbols, understood by everyone involved. I find that anything very sophisticated just gets in the way.

Visualize The Consistency Behind
The Actions of People and Organizations

It came to me during a time when I was working with a multimillionaire. I had worked with him on an occasional basis for years. Over all this time he had exhibited a lot of very strange behavior. In the early years, before he had made his money, we thought he was weird, but when he became rich, he was just eccentric. With a laugh and a shrug, people he worked with would explain his sometimes-strange behavior as a result of sunspot activity or tight shorts.

Then while attending a meeting with this man, I saw the reason for his strange behavior. It was a meeting where I didn't have to do anything but be there; my body needed to fill a chair, but my mind could be on Mars. As the meeting progressed, I was doodling on a sheet of paper and suddenly had a flash of insight. I could see the underlying belief that drove all this man's decisions.

I could also see one belief that pretty well summed up how he felt about everything: *MY way is the RIGHT and ONLY way.*

With a few words and images on a note pad the invisible had suddenly become visible. I had strung together a consistent string of responses from the man that could be summarized under the previous belief. I could then visualize the future and the disasters that would be mine if I continued to work with him. I could also see the past and the thread that tied those years of erratic behavior together into a coherent pattern.

Put yourself in my shoes and you can see the power of reading the consistent pattern behind this person I was dealing with. If this person, who has bought totally into this belief, were to join me in a business ven-

ture and the business failed, whose fault would he feel it to have be–his or mine? In any disagreement over management marketing directions (or anything else for that matter), guess who would have the only correct view? As long as that idea was cemented into his brain, could I ever possibly come out on top?

Having that insight was a lifesaver for me economically. After realizing the patterns of his behavior, I broke off my business association with this man. Later I warned others who were involved with this person. Several said: *"Don't get all worked up. Things are going to work out just fine. You've got to be crazy not to go in with us."*

Half a year later the words were, *"How I wish I had listened to you. I thought you were nuts, but I was the one who was crazy. It's one thing to lose a good deal*

↓ *A visual note profiling a person that I was thinking of working with. This page dictated my only logical response–don't get involved.*

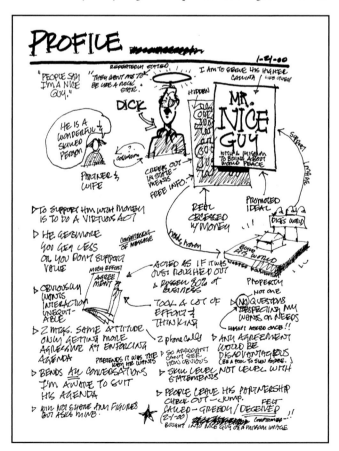

It surprises me how often visual people don't fully use the visual tools that could really provide them with a competitive edge.

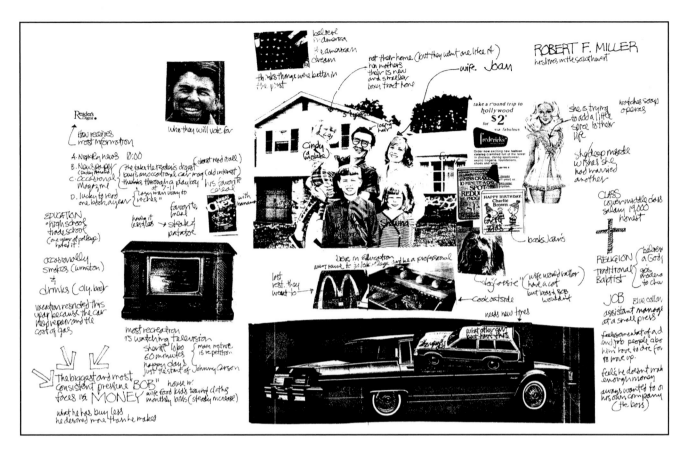

↑ *This sheet is the profile for a marketing meeting reviewing the needs and perception of the intended customer of a proposed product introduction.*

↓ *I even visually profile myself. A page from my visual notes from my journal about a reoccurring dream. Yes, I need my head examined.*

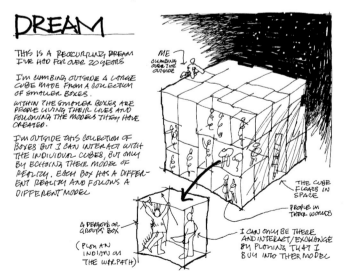

of money if you're wealthy like him, but it is another if you are not."

Every important person or groups that I work with or I'm thinking of working with I create visual notes about them, profiling their often hidden beliefs from the pattern in consistency of their actions. These profile maps have proven to be an essential tool in all of my business dealings, greatly helping me on making decisions, such as the commitment of resources, determining approaches to achieve desire results, how to build a unified direction, and in predicting the final outcomes from various proposed alternatives. I figure that it's better to know something about their perceptions than the usual approach, which is driven by wishful thinking.

↑*A simple visual model illustrating a decision making process that has been taught to over 100,000 people.*

Achieving Understanding From Images

Rapid Visual Information Structuring is at the core of this entire book. Quickly creating visual models to provide an organizing framework for information is the underlying motive behind every idea, concept, and image on these pages. Artists and designers typically see drawing as both an aesthetic and intuitive activity. To them drawing is emotionally driven vehicle that is primarily a means for creative expression. But with the Rapid Visualization approach, drawing is primarily a vehicle for the organization, packaging, and delivering of information.

It doesn't take many brain cells to figure that we now live in the information age. Our daily lives are filling up with increasingly more information. With tapes, CDs, DVD's, hard drives, downloads and updates, journals, reports and web sites, it's also obvious we need something to give order and meaning to all this growing information.

This is where holistic images become powerful and effective devices. Images give order, meaning, and accessibility to all this growing glut of information. Images turn chaotic and disconnected facts into something accessible and usable. Images turn information into knowledge.

I was involved in a series of meetings over some major changes between various competing departments within a company. The purpose of these meetings was to work out with all the key decision makers involved in the reorganization of their various departments. These were awful meetings, some of the worst I'm ever been to, and I've been present at some real doozers.

Between the battle to save one's turf and the struggle to adapt to changing market conditions things weren't going well. These meetings usually started off OK, but it wasn't long before the voices were being raised. Yelling often occurred and emotions ran high. I think there would have been a brawl between the competing parties if their shirts were another color other than white. Then as the hour droned on, everyone fell into a numbing stupor, only to repeat the same sequence the next day.

↓*A model for a parenting program. It's a very simple image that was very difficult to achieve. Sxometimes simple isn't easy. This model took a good deal of testing with the intended audience to finally achieve the results we wanted.*

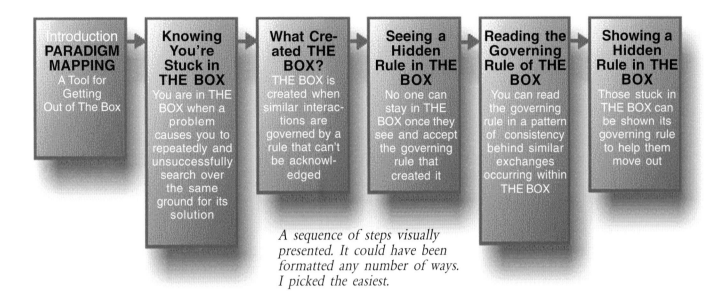

A sequence of steps visually presented. It could have been formatted any number of ways. I picked the easiest.

I could say I saved the day and I did, but at the time I didn't have the slightest idea of what I was doing. In one of these meetings I started to doodle, not for any other higher purpose than I was totally bored and had to do something to avoid falling asleep. Looking back I think I was simply doodling on that note pad just to make some sense from what was really happening in these seemingly endless meetings.

During a potty break, one of the department heads started to read my notes. When I got back into the

↓ *This chart was originally rough, but then refined in a few minutes on a computer.*

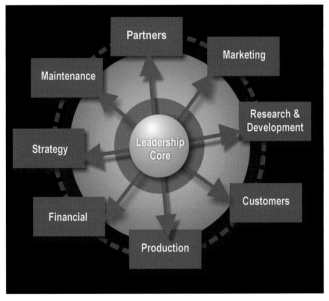

NOTE: These images or visualized knowledge structures typically have no other purpose than to capture in as simple a way as possible the essential order to the information.

room he apologized for taking a peek, but said he liked what I was saying in the notes and asked me to show these notes to everyone else. I didn't mind him looking at my doodles, but I didn't think they would have much value. (This was back when I was young and naive.) But the director insisted and I ended up in front of all the meeting attendees redrawing on a white board my previously scrawled doodles.

The effect these simple images had on everyone in the meeting room was electrifying. It shocked even me, and I was the doodler. Everyone's attention immediately shifted from opposing each other to the front of the room where I was refining and working out the evolving model. Everyone present was unexpectedly working together, jointly creating a unifying image that became a kind of collective meaning for everything that they were facing. Where before there was derision, suddenly there was direction. I was a design director within one of the departments, but that day I was facilitator for a company restructuring, an inadvertent and very enlightening change in occupations. Since then, I seen the same thing happen numerous times. Images have a power to coalesce ideas and information into something people can get a handle on, make some meaning out of it, and utilize the knowledge gained for practical applications.

That power is further enhanced when those visual models are rapidly drawn. People have limited attention spans and the exponential growth of informa-

The validity of any principle, concept, or idea can often best be determined by the results achieved from its application—over time.

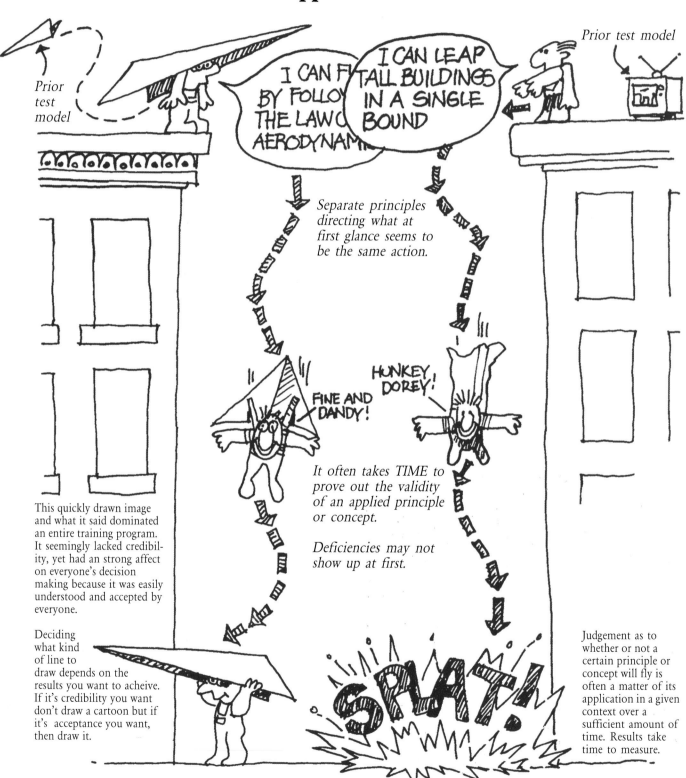

Prior test model

Prior test model

Prior test model

I CAN FLY BY FOLLOWING THE LAW OF AERODYNAMICS

I CAN LEAP TALL BUILDINGS IN A SINGLE BOUND

Separate principles directing what at first glance seems to be the same action.

FINE AND DANDY!

HUNKEY DOREY!

It often takes TIME to prove out the validity of an applied principle or concept.

Deficiencies may not show up at first.

This quickly drawn image and what it said dominated an entire training program. It seemingly lacked credibility, yet had an strong affect on everyone's decision making because it was easily understood and accepted by everyone.

Deciding what kind of line to draw depends on the results you want to acheive. If it's credibility you want don't draw a cartoon but if it's acceptance you want, then draw it.

SPLAT!

Judgement as to whether or not a certain principle or concept will fly is often a matter of its application in a given context over a sufficient amount of time. Results take time to measure.

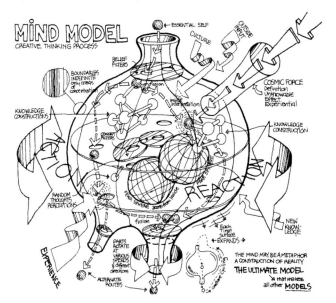

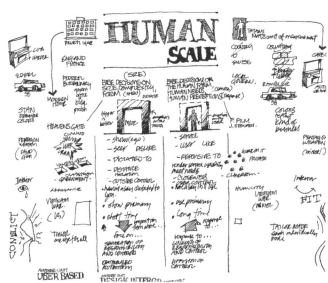

↑ This image of a thinking process got so complicated it failed to explain what a group was trying to say. Maybe in illustrating that complexity it actually succeeded.

↓ An image created to define a need. We all kept floating around until this concept was visually defined.

↑ Notes from my notebook that ended up being used to explain an architectual concept and its application in human resource management.

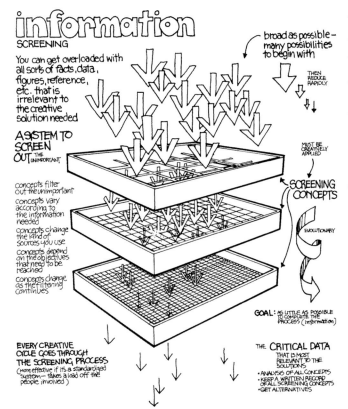

tion is further eroding even that limiting factor. In most situations, understanding and a decision it is needed yesterday. We increasingly don't have the time to wait while images are carefully modeled. Sometimes by the time they are finished it's too late, and with the passage of time, information decays, things change, and people shift. Rapidly visualized information into cohesive models, allowing involvement and participation, have a life and powerful dynamic unique to them.

The purpose of these quick drawings is to create understanding, to push people to choices, and to cause change. They are a means to an end not the end in itself. Highly polished images take time, and increaslingly time is what we don't have.

WARNING: Images can be so powerful that they may give the impression that those presenting them know what they are talking about. They often don't. This can be both a disadvantage and an advantage.

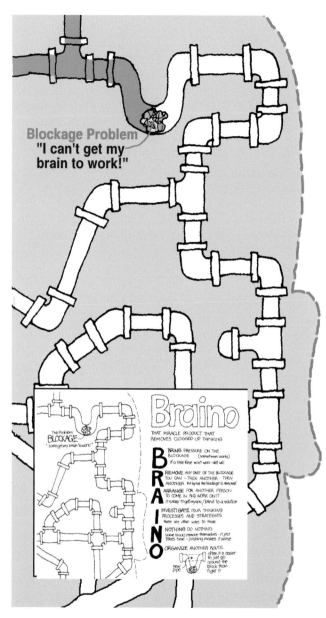

Blockage Problem
"I can't get my brain to work!"

Braino
The Miracle Product That Removes Clogged-Up Thinking

Bring pressure on the Blockage (Sometimes Works!) Then if a little force won't work--alot will theory.

Remove any part of the blockage you can. Then another part and another. Bit by bit it is removed.

Arrange for another person to come in and work on it. It is easy to get myopic or blind to the situation.

Investigate your thinking processes and strategies. There are other ways to think and see the blockage.

Nothing. Do nothing! Some blocks remove themselves. It just takes time and pushing may make matters worse.

Organize another route.

Another Pipe

Often it's easier to just go around the block than fight it.

↖*A metaphorical model for a lecture on innovation. The original drawing is compared with the final one.*

↘*A drawing explaining the function of a heat exchanger. It was first roughed out in pencil then felt pen all on the same sheet of bond paper.*

←*A simple flow diagram became the central idea for the entire form of a building. This is a photo of that model transformed into a three dimensional model.*

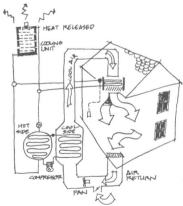

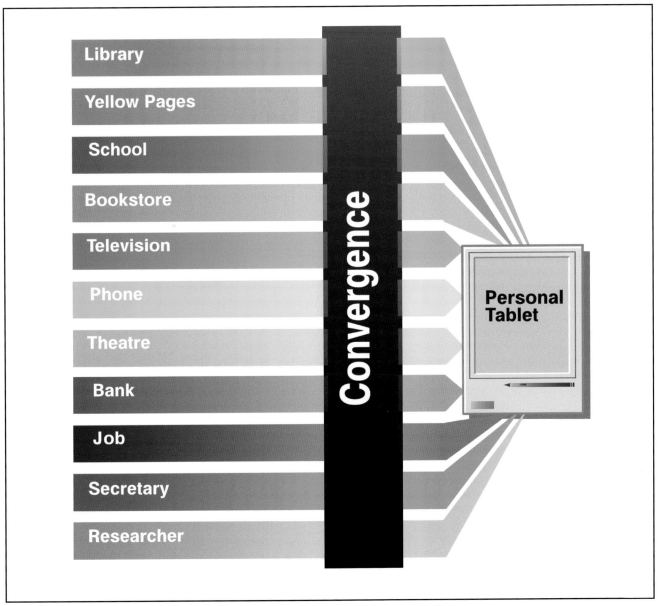

Library

Yellow Pages

School

Bookstore

Television

Phone

Theatre

Bank

Job

Secretary

Researcher

Convergence

Personal Tablet

These images are visual models of information. When you turn information into a visual model you often change information into knowledge.

The top image is of a new computer system, the left image is of a creative principle used in theme park design, and the right drawing is a project management model.

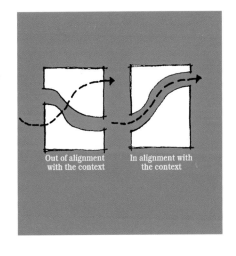

Out of alignment with the context

In alignment with the context

NOTE: We are in the third generation of television watchers. Many of these TV watchers are moving in leadership positions within our society. This is creating a tremendous bias for the visual modeling of information.

Retrieving Complexity From Simplicity

When Mark Twain first started speaking in public his presentations lacked the power and skill that latter made him America's top lecturer. What made the difference were little drawings that he made on small pieces of paper. When he first started he jotted down the usual notes, but later discovered what worked extremely well were little images of the keys points that he wanted to make in his talk, stick-like figures that triggered his mind into capturing the attention of his audience.

Just as with Mark Twain, you can use your own drawn symbols or icons to trigger your mind into the meaning and understanding that icons represent. The icons you construct for yourself are links to more complex knowledge and information that you need to access.

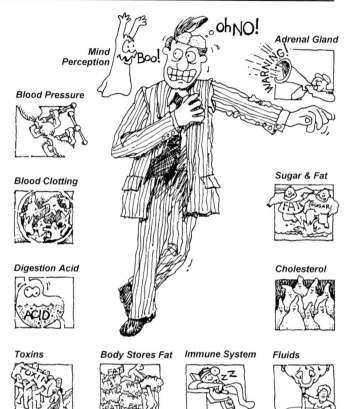

↑ This is a series of icons I developed for someone else. It was for a presentation on stress reduction to business managers.

A visually minded person can use a symbol or icon library of their own drawings to help them access key information easier and faster.

This simple image of tape is the link to much more complex information.

← Here are some of my own icons (with even more on the next page) linked to my more detailed and involved notes. These symbols have meaning for me and they serve as a memory device to recall more detailed information.

Since we are all drowning in information, this simple tool can help sus get some much needed air.

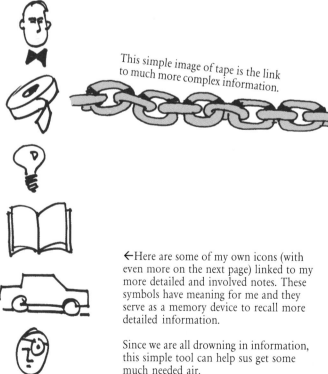

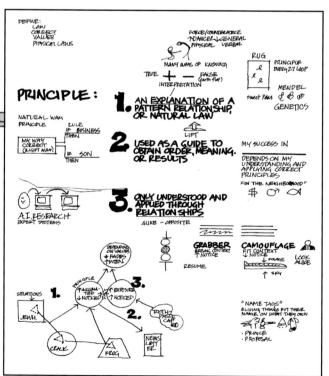

NOTE: It's surprising, after so many years. When I collected a page of
my icons to show you, I still remember what they all represent.

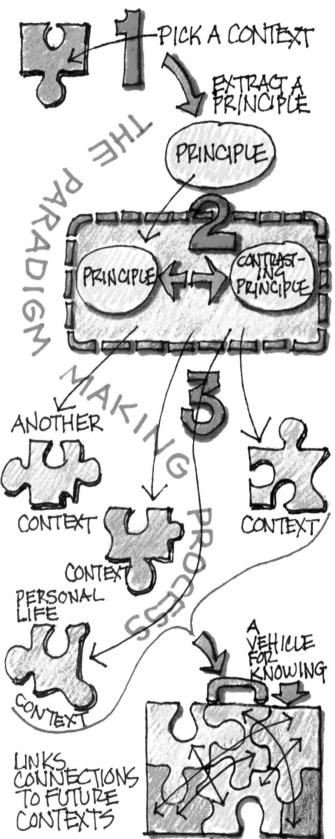

PICK A CONTEXT

EXTRACT A PRINCIPLE

PRINCIPLE

PRINCIPLE ⟷ CONTRASTING PRINCIPLE

THE PARADIGM MAKING PROCESS

ANOTHER

CONTEXT

CONTEXT

CONTEXT

PERSONAL LIFE

CONTEXT

A VEHICLE FOR KNOWING

LINKS CONNECTIONS TO FUTURE CONTEXTS

A Uniquely Designerly Way of Knowing

While teaching college classes and developing business training programs, the one thing that I recognized was how ineffective traditional teaching methods can be. In school, hours upon hours are spent memorizing facts to pass some test—then to be later forgotten. In the business world, people attend one seminar or conference after another wherein promises of improved performance are always high and results are typically very low.

But there are unique designerly ways of knowing that could improve all this training and schooling. I've always been amazed at the variety and complexity of the problems designers deal with and resolve. I'm an industrial designer by training and I've been in many different situations where clients drop their problem on me to solve, often one I have never seen before. I then take their problem, struggle with it and apply a designer's problem-solving methods, attitude, and drawing skills, and then solve it. Sometimes the solution even surprises me, how well it works (of course, I never tell the clients about my surprise). I've seen other designers of all types do the very same thing. If you could pull out at least some of the design processes that allow designers to do this and teach it to others, you could drastically improve their ability to learn and adapt to change.

I've done a good deal of exhibit and museum work, and at the beginning of these projects, the beginning research step is was always the same. I get a table stacked to the ceiling with data, research, books, and reports, far too much information and knowledge to effectively grasp or even read in the allotted time.

Situations like these demanded that I develop a more effective (designerly) way of dealing with all this information. So with drawings, diagrams, and a general systems way of seeing things, I created a process that works extremely well in structuring a coherent and communicable pattern for this stack of information.

I knew this process was working when I found myself in a meeting where a paleontologist, a geologist, a ecologist, a civil engineer, a curator, a soil expert (whatever they are called), an organic chemist, and so on, were present, a group too diverse to ever be together naturally. But my visual notes and drawings on the board and the paper became the medium of communication between all of them. Since then I've used this design methods of structuring and communicating information into knowledge in over 60 museums, several books, and numerous educational projects.

A Powerful New Way of Teaching The Frameworks For Knowledge

At first, I used this process only on my own projects. After more time and refinement, I shared it in-house within the firms I worked. It made doing all these information-laden projects much easier to accomplish and more effective in achieving their objectives. This process gave a competitive edge to anyone who used it. Years later, I gave this process the name *Relational Learning* and started using it as an improved teaching and learning approach. I even started to get revenge with all the bad teachers I've had over the years and taught it to interested educators who achieved some very exciting results from their students.

For example, to test this new training approach, I took Relational Learning into a multi-cultural class at a university. The class instruction involved teaching non-Americans about American history. After the classes were over, foreign students ended up teaching American students their own history. There was also a consistent unity and clarity occurring among the incredible variety of students involved. Some other results were absolutely mystical in their effects. I tested this method again in a new business training company. I helped developed their training for a time management course which proved extremely successful. This company is now one of the largest business training companies in the country. In every situation I have used this approach with similar successful results.

It is basically a system of instruction that teaches through visualization the conceptual frameworks or paradigms underlying any subject matter or area of expertise. Once these underlying knowledge frameworks are taught—along with a process of linking facts and other data to it—a minimum of additional instruction is needed and updating the instruction is easy and quick. →

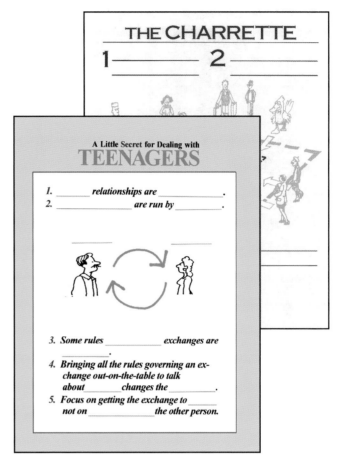

↑ *Two single sheet workbooks from classes on how to having a successful charrette and how to be a more effective parent.*

↓ *Visual paradigms or models like these have been taught to many groups all over the world with the same unique results.*

Human minds are naturally wired to be visual learners and with the increase in the visual media this is even more so.

Relational Learning

Relational Learning utilizes knowledge critical to the survival of an organization and the competence of an individual. It is taught in a minimum amount of time using limited resources. It creates understandable new learning structures or paradigms that are rapidly updated and have a significant positive long-term impact.

Relational Learning is a natural, whole-brain approach to learning and thinking. This approach, when learned, causes a dramatic change in how a person acquires knowledge and perceives life's situations. Through this framework-building process, people see that a multitude of situations and contexts have value for solving their personal problems and dealing with their cares, decisions, hopes, and expectations. Using this process people typically have the experience of the *ah-ha!* feeling of excitement when they make a great discovery, gain a sudden deep understanding of a subject, or when they find something that really works for them.

The Relational Learning process expands what you know into a more effective foundation of usable knowledge. Once acquired, a learner can use this process for the rest of their life to more efficiently obtain whatever they desire. Relational Learning is for people whose job demands immediate application of the right knowledge. It is for people who don't have time to repeatedly spend hours away from the job in seminars and workshops intended to help them adapt to a rapidly changing environment. This approach to teaching is for the new world of information, where adapting to change is crucial for survival, where continual learning is the constant demand, and where time is often the most important commodity.

How To Teach or Learn Relationally
What follows is the process in a nutshell. It is more complex than this, but what follows will give you its basic components and steps.

1 Choose A Context, Event, Situation, or Subject Matter Pick any subject, but context-rich subjects tend to work the best, such as history or natural science. It can even be an event in your life that just happened or a situation that is pressing on your mind for some reason. The context selected will be taught in two ways: This process is taught primarily and the subject is secondary. Relational Learning can't be taught separate from any context though. It is a process like tennis or singing where you need have a court or a stage to actually do it. It is not content like math or chemistry. And like any other process, you learn it by repeatedly doing it under the direction of a good coach or teacher.

2 Extract And State A Principle or Generalized Concept From This Context Pull out from the context selected a statement of the principle or concept in operation, one that explains the patterns in the context. For example, if it's chemical reaction, pull out the principle of a catalyst; or if it's a certain war, the concept of defense and advance or if it's grandpa, why he repeatedly tells the very same stories.

Also include the principle or concept's opposite or contrasting statement. This helps refine and define the chosen concept. It's interesting how seeing something's opposite, like seeing the negative space in art, improves understanding of the thing that is generating its opposite.

The concept's statement is always done in two languages. This increases the linkage between all the contexts you are dealing with. Writing and simple quick drawings are the languages that I find most effective. This is not complicated, just an odd thing to do from the usual approach to learning, and it's usually done on just a single sheet of paper.

3 Link This Principle To A Variety of Other Contexts In other words, find the same principle and its opposite in other subject matters, such as chemistry, geology, or dance. For example, a principle taken from a historical context was linked to a physical science, such a geology. The principle is also linked in words and images with this multitude of other contexts. The most important link is always the students or learner's own personal life.

Secrets From An Information Designer

Learning this process basically accomplishes two things. First it gives a structure or framework of understanding for the subject being taught. These structures are the essence of memory, causing the content that is learned when using this process to become unforgettable.

Doing this process also brings the paradigm or conceptual framework-making process of person or the group out of something that was typically subconscious into full awareness. I've found that paradigms, especially what I call governing paradigms, dominate and direct all our decision making. Having this paradigm-making process obvious and skill-based dramatically shifts the decision making process of any student learning it.

Our world is in an ever-worsening pickle because of people's choices seems like a simple enough concept—improve people's decision making process and the world will improve. This Relational Learning process has been tried on all levels of learning, from the primary grades through college and on into professional training. The results have been the same—a dramatic shift in thinking, perceiving, and understanding.

↓When teaching a subject's paradigm with Relational Learning you don't need to use anything very sophisticated, nothing more complicated than a single sheet of paper that is sequentially filled in by the student throughout the class. The test? Just the same blank sheet to see what can be recalled by filling it in again.

Rapidly constructed images built sequentially in front of an interested audience can magically communicate some deep insights.

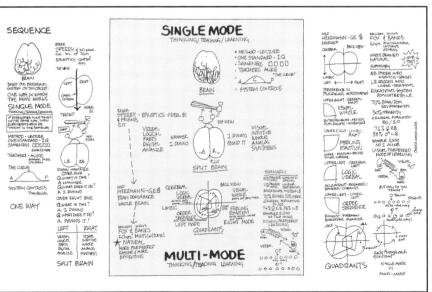

Optimizing Time and Impact

There's a designer who prides himself in the fact that he doesn't use a computer. "My designs and drawings are still hand-done," he proudly states to anyone who will listen. I suppose if he was around at the time paper was invented he would also state that his designs and drawings are still done in the tried and proven method of drawing on rocks.

I also know an illustrator who prides herself in never using anything but a computer. "Paper is essentially obsolete. All my illustrations are pixels and bytes from start to finish. I paint with light. Pigment is only for house and portrait painters," she likes to say.

Personally, I belong in the middle of these two extremes. Pad, paper, mouse, and keyboard are all tools to use in getting the job done. My view of the computer and imaging software fits under the following rules.

1 **Ideal Versus What-Cha-Really-Got** A computer is very seductive. It can get you believing that it is faster and better than you are. With perfect images, a computer tricks you into believing your hand-done drawings won't work better. If you buy this you may reach the point where you can't even do a single drawing without using all the necessary perfection-making electronic equipment. Yes, it's all fast and perfect. But the perfection is often a disguise for the superficial and the speed it promotes is often a total con.

Try timing how fast computers are really getting things done. In one recent project, I timed how long it took a designer to visualize a project. It took forever. He never did get it done. He spent all his time trying to learn his new software. I took pen to paper to finish the needed images for the project. He never did produce any drawings.

Too often we get caught up in all the promotion about computers and the latest software, not stopping to really take a good hard look at what they really accomplish. As a general rule, I try seeing what I really know and can really do with a computer before I ever put aside the pen and paper.

2 **Making Drawings Faster and Easier** A computer really helps move things along faster and easier in combination with hands-on drawing skills. When hand and computer are working together, they benefit and interact with each other.

Nothing yet can beat the speed, dynamics, and intimacy achieved when pen hits paper as you're brainstorming along. But the more complex and replicable the drawings get no pen can beat the speed and refinement of the machine.

My drawings are a combination of tools with the overarching guideline being whichever is faster and easier. I find the beginnings of a drawing are better left to pen and paper, and the ending of a drawing is better left to the machine.

These movie set elevations were first rapidly sketched on paper then scanned into a computer to correct, modify, and add some color.

3 **Fixing The Imperfections of Life** Technology fixes mistakes better than any hand tool ever thought of. You can arrange, then rearrange, and arrange again, fixing a warped perspective and changing one element into another. Modifying, bending, refining, and removing the images are possible, even easy to do, with a computer. I now fix my mistakes in ways I never thought of as possible with white-out or a kneaded eraser.

This drawing has undergone so many computerized reincarnations, which would have been impossible to do by hand, that I've forgotten where its first life began.

4 **That Little Something Extra** Adjusting color, tone, balance, contrast, arrangement, and scale on a computer can greatly enhance an image. Plus, if your modification doesn't work you can go back and try something else.

Again, another place a computer can shine is in the enhancing and improving of a drawing. I especially like that it does this so immediately. You can test out what will happen if you change some little thing, all without damaging the original. Never has there been so much visual flexibility at a movement of your fingertips.

5 **When Production Time Arrives** The computer totally dominates when the creative first half of many visualizations ends and the production of those images into various formats occurs.

I remember wishing for a computer program that would do certain things, having specific functions that I was very particular about. I even drew out on paper what these almost magical abilities I really wished I had would look like. Here it is:

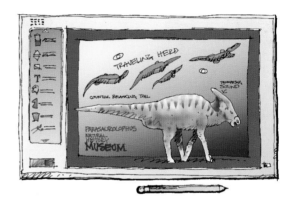

Computers with once only dreamed-of abilities are now commonplace. The rapid visualization of ideas can be dramatically improved and the capabilities greatly expanded when utilizing a computer. But the crucial interactions between the hand, the eye, and the mind of a visualizer, or between others and visualizers, is where the creative essence will originate.

I know the solution is here someplace, but I've repeatedly looked everywhere.

again and again for a seemingly obvious solution that is never found. Do any of these examples sound familiar?

Ann again remarries the same man only this time with a different face and name.

After years of failure, the Sanford's try again with their troubled son who stays troubled.

Despite the implementation of a variety of successful programs used by other companies to curb employee theft, the increase in corporate stealing continues.

A department won't live up to its obvious possibilities, even with another change in leadership, improvement in the quality of teams involved, still more finances, and a move to new offices.

In all the years I've served as a consultant this has been my biggest problem—getting people to move out of their boxes. Seeing this, I've developed a tool to effectively get people and organizations out of their boxes and moving forward. Here is an introduction to this tool with its three principles.

1 You are in THE BOX when a problem causes you to repeatedly and unsuccessfully search the same ground for its solution.
Being *stuck-in-the-box* is the term used for the inability to resolve obviously solvable problems that don't get solved. These problems remain defiantly free from

Getting Our of The Box
I've watched a company slowly slide itself into insignificance. It once dominated its industry, but now its impact, as well as its stock, is a fraction of what it once was. Recently, another new CEO again tried to implement some much-needed change. One third of the employees were let go. Millions in new capital was invested. The entire structure of the company was dramatically altered to improve productivity and capture new opportunities.

Yet after the smoke cleared from all of these activities, and the sound dimmed from all the motivational talks and chanting of buzzwords, nothing fundamental ever changed. Behind declarations of dramatic and lasting change, people in this company still continue with the same habitual behavior of the past. One manager said to me, "With all this movement around here you would think something would actually move!" Everyone in this company is now deep inside something called *The Box*.

Stuck in The Box
Like the people in this company, we all get stuck in The Box, frantically searching over the same ground

We must redouble our efforts and find the answer!

any solution, all the while soaking up an enormous amount of our time, energy, and other resources. When our solutions don't work, we say to ourselves, "I must not have the right solution or it wasn't implemented correctly." So we redouble our efforts running in endless circles. We are stuck in The Box.

2 THE BOX is created when similar interactions or exchanges are governed by a rule that can't be acknowledged.

All relationships and interactions are exchanges and these exchanges are run by rules. A governing rule is the over-arching rule that directs, defines, and limits a set of exchanges. When a governing rule can't be acknowledged by the people it affects, this generates a rigid and confining situation of preset exchanges that form The Box. These hidden rules block searching in more fruitful locations, thus denying even the possibility of finding a real and effective solution.

Here are two statements from people in two separate companies that have hidden rules embedded within them (not hard to see, but totally impossible to bring to their owner's attention): *"We couldn't possibly be missing those funds because of theft. The director is the most honest man I know." "We must show our clients our innovative leadership and do all phases of this showcase project in-house."* Both comments contain hidden and unacknowledged rules that restrict the abilities of these companies in finding effective resolutions to their most pressing problems.

3 Anyone can get out of THE BOX once they see and accept the governing rule creating it.

An essential part of any search for solutions by people stuck in The Box is the hidden governing rule that invisibly directs the search for any solutions. A problem that repeatedly defies the finding of a solution, typically never consciously includes the hidden rule that is being followed when searching for its solution. When the usually invisible governing rule that is directing the situation is made visible, things automatically change. When an individual or group sees and accepts this formerly hidden rule, they invariably have a fundamental shift in perception and thinking. They must move out of their box.

I know a silly parlor game where one person goes out of a room full of people. Those left collectively select something in the room. The person returns to the room and tries to guess what was selected while a moderator asks the group questions. This pretender always guesses correctly. The others try to come up with the secret on how the fake psychic was so uncannily accurate. Nobody comes up with the answer. As the moderator asks, "Is it the piano? Is it the black dog? How about the vase?" The psychic is following a simple hidden rule: after the first thing the moderator points out that begins with the letter B, it is always the very next thing he points out with a question. For example: If the moderator asks, "Is it the Black dog?" Then, because it begins with the letter B, it will be the very next thing he asks about that was secretly selected—the vase. Geniuses can flounder and fail on this one.

Interestingly, once you know this rule you can never really play this absurd game again. It is the same with seeing a formerly hidden governing rule. Once you know and accept what it is, you can't keep playing the same way—you can't stay in The Box. →

PARADIGM MAPPING: A tool to show people inside THE BOX its hidden governing rule

Paradigm Mapping is the method I've used to get people to clearly see and to accept the hidden rules that govern their exchanges and move them out of The Box. A visual representation of a person's or group's hidden rules are constructed in front of them. By using quickly-made images with accompanying notation and continual input from the viewers, what is formerly unconscious is now brought into awareness.

Let me show you how this is done. A facilitator puts words and images on a large white board in front of everyone involved. He becomes their hands, jogs their minds, calms egos, clarifies, etc. While this process is happening, the facilitator is erasing, correcting, questioning, and refining until a final consensus is reached that what they are viewing is their governing rule. Seeing everything slowly develop and evolved before them dramatically increases their ownership and acceptance of what is written on the board, greatly improving the chance for new insightsz.

To effectively visualize another's rules, the facilitator creating the image must concentrate on reading the consistent pattern behind peoples' exchanges, then graphically summarize and represent that pattern. These images need to reflect back to the viewers what they are communicating and agreeing to. Also, the images are simple and symbolic (using sophisticated drawings or images can get in the way by hindering easy participation). Attention is focused on the image, not on each other or the facilitator. Visually represented, everyone can see which rules are dominating

A hidden governing rule is visualized and brought out into the open. If it's accepted, a shift occurs to going outside the box

A simple visualization of the mind-shifting process that happens when using Paradigm Mapping.

Hmmm . .

THAT'S IT!

Paradigm Mapping works best on individuals or small groups/teams. Larger groups are too unwieldy.

their interactions and exchanges. They can have an understanding of what has locked them in their box.

I once worked with a woman on a job where we had to manage a number of ongoing projects. I quite liked her, but she had one habit that kept getting in the way of us effectively doing our jobs. She continually brought up the issue of 'unfairness' to women. She had been poorly treated in the past, had seen other women have similar problems, and wanted to do something about it.

The projects we had to finish had absolutely nothing to do with this issue. The time needed other places was being spent as a forum to further her cause. Finally something had to be done to focus on the projects at hand. The buck was passed and it ended up on my lap.

Two questions written out (only to her) on a white board was all it took. The first one was, "Have you ever seen me discriminate against a woman in any manner?" The second question was, "What does fairness-to-women have to do with finishing these projects?" Then I left for home. I didn't need her to literally answer them for me. Behind these two questions was the rule of a box she was attempting to put our entire team in. To her credit, everything immediately improved.

In another story, a company went through quite a trauma. The corporate president/chairman left with his secretary for an extended trip to the Caribbean with $24 million of the company's funds. Nobody in the company missed the secretary, but they really missed the $24 million. Struggling for months and months for survival, if ever an organization had to redefine itself, it was this one.

After more than half a year, everyone in the company settled down after accepting the shock of what happened. They had also stabilized their financial situation. Then they faced the serious problem of redefining themselves, finally asking those hard questions like "Who we are?" and "What are we about?"

I was called in to help them in this redefining process. I had done some design work for them and in working on the design problems they saw my conceptual skills and pulled me into some top-level meetings to redesign their company. I then proceeded to completely waste one top management session just letting everyone vent (to a safe outsider) all of his or her hurt and frustration at what had recently happened. It was really quite emotional and the only thing I could do was just listen. But the next session a week later was much more effective.

In this meeting I quickly laid out visually where they were going, what had happened, and possible future options. After an hour or so of interaction with my next step, things took a new turn. I visually laid out to them their present beliefs about how things should work and stepped aside to the wall. Immediately there was an argument with yelling and anger. Nobody was sitting anymore.

After the yelling and high emotions subsided, came the apologies and then somethingquite interesting happened. I suppose the yelling was everyone getting all their frustration out. When they could see that their real emotions were OK and that everyone was hurt in some way, things changed.

Next to an icon on the white board, which indicated everyone there, a simple sentence was written by a vice president. The group immediately coalesced into →

SANCE 2002

APRIL 29

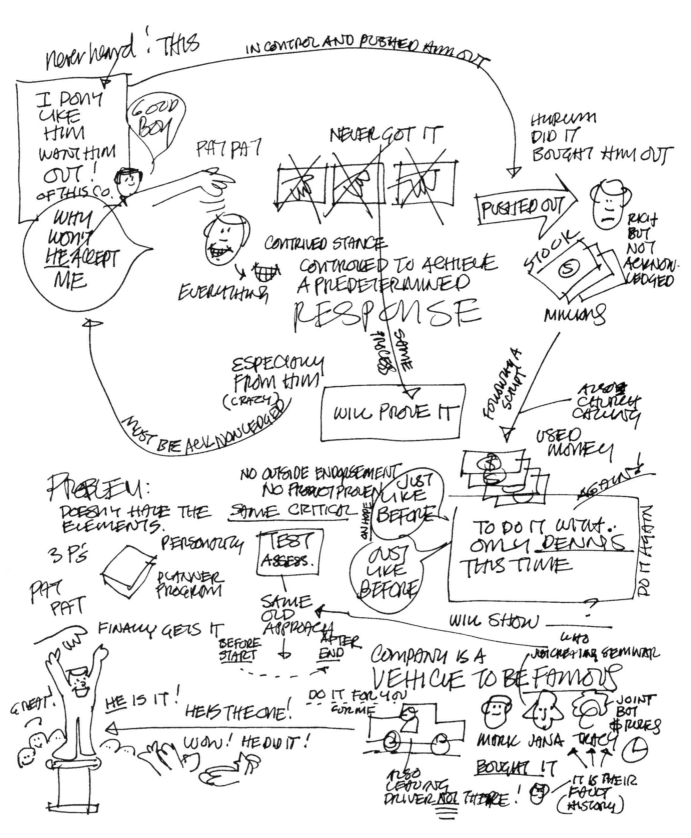

a new team with a goal that had new meaning for everyone. It was almost physically jolting in how fast this happened. Everyone was very ready for what they most wanted.

I have a confession; I often don't have the foggiest idea what is going to happen in these Paradigm Mapping sessions. The dynamics of these sessions with everyone questioning and contributing is just too complex to have the slightest prophetic insight. With this one, I was totally in the dark. But everyone loved what had been done. Now with the firm back on solid ground, I'm locked into the company's culture and mythology as the man who "turned their company around."

In still another story, I was consulting for a company that had been diligently working on the same problem for months. The people in this company had tried everything. "We just haven't found the right solution yet," is what they kept saying.

As an outsider, I had the advantage. I wasn't yet tainted by all of the diligent effort. I could see the one place they hadn't looked was at the over-arching rule they were following to resolve the situation. They had looked at everything else too many times.

They were trying to expand their services, but didn't have enough money to make the necessary improvements. They had accomplished a lot. Things had just reached the point where they needed money and only more money would work. The rule that wasn't being openly dealt with was that the company leadership wasn't giving them the needed cash.

I found myself drawing concentric circles and stick figures on a couple of large white boards in the conference room. I visually showed them how they saw their problem, and their attempted solutions. Then they collectively saw a solution—they were solving the wrong problem. Their real problem wasn't the customer, but their corporate leadership. Their bosses were not seeing the value in what this department was attempting to do. They needed to do a sales job on the higher-ups.

The department head stated that he never saw a meeting get so focused in such a short time with just a few scribbles and rough notes. He said, "You doing this, whatever it is, was instrumental in us resolving a problem that had remained totally immovable. I even watched my own people come up with effective solutions when the day before they were mentally frozen!"

Perhaps you can use Paradigm Mapping to help someone you know get out of their box. Give it a try. Seeing what was formerly invisible can often cause quite a shift. It may surprise you what happens.

← *This is a genuine paradigm map, They always look the same—confusing. They never make any real sense to anyone, but the session's participants.*

The Creative Power Behind, "Once Upon a Time . . . "

Shep was an old dog and he suffered more each added day he lived. He was more than just an animal; he was one of the family. We had all grown up with Shep, shared our hopes and dreams with him, and cried our tears to his kind face.

The family could see and feel the pain in his eyes, and that was too much—it was time. Dad couldn't do it. He said, "It's like one of the kids." So the buck was passed and I was left alone with the inevitable task. I loaded my gun and climbed on the horse. And just as Shep had done thousands of times before, the old dog followed along.

After we had passed over a couple of hills away from the house, I found a place to put him out of his misery. While still on the horse, I took aim as the dog circled down below. I slowly squeezed the trigger, which seemed incredibly stiff. The gun fired when the dog crossed in front of the horse, then I suddenly fell to the ground with the horse on top of me. I had shot the horse in the neck!

That walk back home was more painful for me than it ever was for old Shep, who followed along behind.

Illustration from a collection of stories all generated from an underlying story about a professor's lifelong research project into myths.

The stories behind the movies created at special tours at studios are all about how movies are made and famous actors who worked on bringing those stories to life.

The dog you saw in this story was different from the one I saw. The hills were different from the ones I imagined, yet we both created an image of what happened.

We imagine in our heads a more complete picture than words and images alone could ever tell.

In human societies all over the world and throughout time, stories have had power. They are the driving forces to much of what we do. Stories about what who we are, stories from the past, imagined and real stories, all provide a kind of mental rack for us to hang meaning, giving our lives a sense of structure and purpose. And the most important stories are the ones in our heads and the ones you often never hear.

I used to work at a motion picture studio and one of the most important concepts I learned there was the idea of a backstory. A backstory is the story behind the story, the story you never hear or see, but is the driving force to a film. It's the larger story where all the other stories, images, words, scenes, and shots in a film are derive from.

One of the best examples of the use of a backstory is at Skywalker Ranch, the George Lucas offices and production studio located in a beautiful valley in Northern California. The buildings in this unique working environment are made to look like a winery and ranch.

All choices on placement and design of the buildings were driven by a backstory about a certain family.

The underlying unity and beauty of the environment and the consistency of the design choices were all derived from a simple made-up story.

In working on a project, the Smokey Bear Visitor Center, I used the story of the little burnt bear called Smokey and the idea that became an icon for fire prevention to design the very structure of the building and the flow of all the exhibits' content.

Herein lies a little secret to drawing—get the story first, then do the drawings. The story becomes a wellspring of ideas and concepts to use in generating the images on paper. Maybe only you know the story. But while others grope for ideas you'll have more than a steady supply.

Jungle Rescue

↓In designing theme parks the central core of the entire process is the telling and retelling of stories.

DC-2 sircraft made to look like it crashed. (Already purchased!)

A radio is on with frantic requests for location and the plane's status.

Features an elaborate background story the guest can interact with.

Corporate sponsorship.

Flight 291 to Cape Town has crashed! After desperate messages for help the plane's radio has gone dead. The plane is down but no word on what has happened to the 12 passengers or the crew of three. On board were the mysterious scientist Dr. F. T. Fertenswerger, the famous movie star couple Stone Waters and Cynthia Summerhayes, two sisters from the Lady-of-the-Lake Convent in Durban, local businessman Wendal Maas, and six other passengers. Captain John Doven, an experienced pilot, was on his last flight home to marry Tracy Cadishson of the wealthy socialite family.

The DC-2 is believed to have gone down near the Lost River. Even after repeated attempts to locate the downed aircraft, no word has been heard of anyone on the airplane since the last radio message was cut short. Rescue efforts have been called off, but the Cadishson Family now has offered a million rand reward to anyone locating survivors.

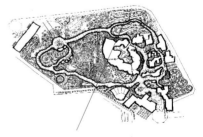

Location

Steps to Task Mapping

Today managers of all types face a proliferation of "elephants." Massive and important, they are dropped on a manager's desk late Friday afternoon and they are expected to be meticulously dissected, carefully prepared, and ready to eat on Monday morning. Task Mapping, a proven recipe for dividing elephants into digestible pieces, will teach you to organize long-range or short-term tasks so that they are easier to plan, managed better, and turn out ultimately more consumable.

End First

While it may sound strange, the recipe for Task Mapping begins by visualizing the end results first, in other words, seeing the elephant in its ready-to-eat stage. How does it smell, look, and taste? Will you serve elephant steak or stew? Of the African, Indian, or Asiatic variety? Where and when will you serve it? How many will partake of the delicacy? Will you need recipe copies for possible purchasing agents, or are you planning simply to freeze it as a solution to the rise in meat prices?

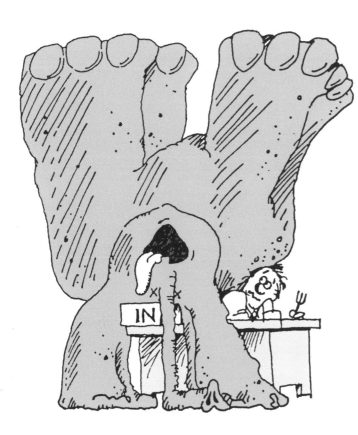

To visualize the end results, you must be able to project into the future the definition and exact details of the desired outcome.

Time Line

Next, estimate how much time the entire process will take—for example, from obtaining and preparing an elephant to washing the dishes after eating it. This figure should be put on a visible time line. This time line will vary depending on the project to be accomplished. For instance, if elephants live in your backyard, your time line will be much shorter than for someone who must schedule a safari to Africa to find an animal. This figure is only a projected estimate, and the time line may change and evolve as you follow your own task mapping process.

Chunks

Breaking the entire project into big chunks is the next step. Divisions exist in any process, so watch for the natural crack lines. For example, after eating dinner,

How Do You Eat an Elephant?
And How That Relates to Visualizing the Completion of a Complex Task

Everyone knows the answer to that question—one bite at a time. But how does one reduce the elephant into those bite-size pieces?

The next few pages present the process of *Task Mapping,* a planning tool to help break our project elephants into more palatable pieces, to organize the immense and seemingly endless tasks we receive daily, into smaller sizes that are easier to manage.

Task Mapping is a planning tool. It breaks the steps of accomplishing a task into a visual schematic or map, making scheduling, assigning resources, and plotting progress much easier. This is a lighthearted introduction to this project management process.

Putting time constraints on your task makes it more realistic and helps you see the inherent problems and possibilities involved in accomplishing the task.

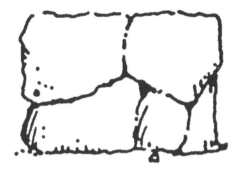

Every project has natural divisions which can be divided into separate tasks to be more easily accomplished.

Shift Smaller

Repeat steps 3 and 4 with the existing chunks. Divide every large chunk into smaller chunks. Prepare a list of each task that needs to be accomplished with each large chunk. Write them on individual slips of paper for quick adjustments. Shifting to smaller and smaller chunks will allow you to really sink your teeth into the tasty morsels. Projects can be made more digestible by cutting them into pieces.

we stand up from the table and do the dishes. After quartering a carcass, a butcher naturally begins to section the beef pieces. Not all tasks have such obvious crack lines, but when a change in function occurs while you are accomplishing a task, identify each distinct function as a separate chunk.

Failure to dissect a project into large chunks can cause confusion and poor performance. For instance, one boss who had been without a secretary for six weeks, immediately put her new secretary to work. "Start there," she said, pointing to an immense, unorganized pileup of paper. Unaware of any natural crack lines or chunks, the secretary began "gulping" up the piles. The first hour was disastrous—the following two, worse. At the end of the day, the boss met with her assistants. "I'm afraid we've made a bad mistake," she said. "This secretary is totally incompetent."

The boss would have seen dramatically different results had she given some hints as to the natural crack lines: "Divide this mess into the accounts payable, receivable, and general correspondence," she could have said. The secretary's work, no doubt, would have progressed in a more efficient manner.

Sequence

The fourth step to Task Mapping is arranging the big chunks in a sequential order. If in your own project two or more large chunks must be accomplished at the same time, just place them at the same point on the time line. For instance, the secretary could have begun with the accounts payable, then moved on to the accounts receivable. Or after prioritizing each pile by arranging it in chronological order, she could have worked on the piles concurrently.

In scaling down, you may want to consider the following:

Focus on the relationships between the tasks.

Draw arrows between tasks to show the best sequence.

Divide which tasks that are done sequentially (one after the other) or must be done simultaneously.

Decide who should accomplish each task.

Find out what is the longest time line that has been defined and then decide if it can it be accomplished with the time required by the final deadline.

Layout

Starting with the last big chunk, lay out every big chunk in sequential order from the end to the beginning. Then lay out the small chunks in sequential order and place them inside the large chunks to which they belong. Because you have worked backward, when all the pieces are in place you should have a backwards task map. Flip-flop the whole map so that it reads from beginning to end. Now you are ready to put the map in its final form, such as the schematic or report.→

Task Mapping

Here is a possible task map to use in developing our plan for eating an elephant.

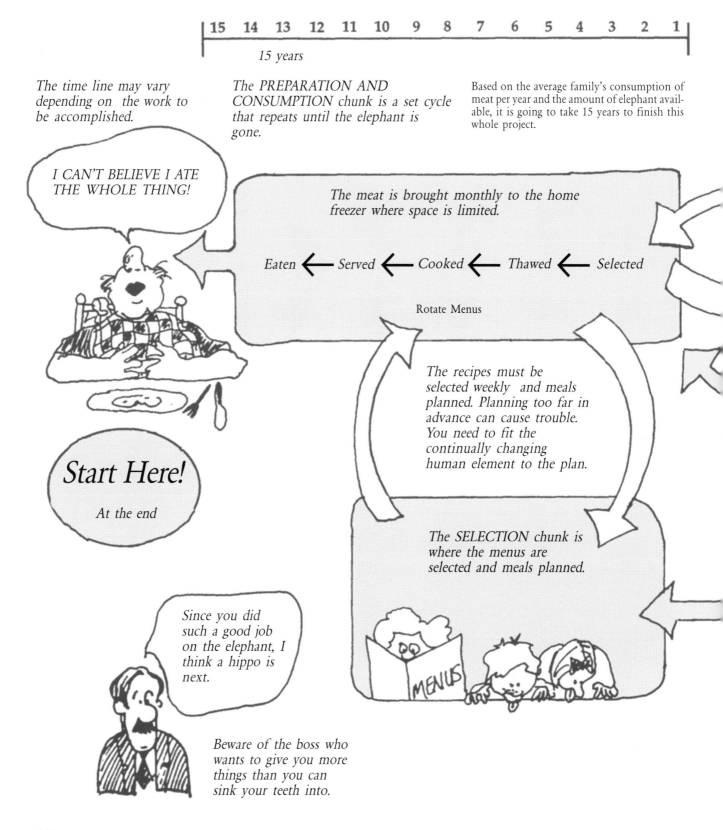

| 15 | 14 | 13 | 12 | 11 | 10 | 9 | 8 | 7 | 6 | 5 | 4 | 3 | 2 | 1 |

15 years

The time line may vary depending on the work to be accomplished.

The PREPARATION AND CONSUMPTION chunk is a set cycle that repeats until the elephant is gone.

Based on the average family's consumption of meat per year and the amount of elephant available, it is going to take 15 years to finish this whole project.

I CAN'T BELIEVE I ATE THE WHOLE THING!

The meat is brought monthly to the home freezer where space is limited.

Eaten ← Served ← Cooked ← Thawed ← Selected

Rotate Menus

Start Here!

At the end

The recipes must be selected weekly and meals planned. Planning too far in advance can cause trouble. You need to fit the continually changing human element to the plan.

The SELECTION chunk is where the menus are selected and meals planned.

Since you did such a good job on the elephant, I think a hippo is next.

MENUS

Beware of the boss who wants to give you more things than you can sink your teeth into.

The BIG SECRET to this entire technique is organizing everything backwards. When you communicate the plan to someone else, just reverse the order.

24 HOURS

End Here!
At the beginning

7 6 5 4 3 2 1

1 week

1 day

The PROCESSING chunk is the step when you freeze the elephant. It needs to be preserved during the time needed to do the subsequent steps. This is going to take a week.

The PREPARATION chunk is where it's cut up and shipped to the packing plant to be frozen. Time is critical here.

Money needed ← Frozen ← Organize packages

Cut and transport ← Convince packer ← Call meat packer

This must be done in 24 hours.

When they stop laughing, proceed to the next step.

What do you mean it's all in hamburger? I'll need a second mortgage to pay for it all!

HA! HA! HA! HA! HA!

The DROP THE NEWS chunk is here. You tell the family what they're going to eat for the next few years.

Tell them how healthy Africans are.

Drop the news ← Explain advantages ← Call a family meeting

Do it gently!

Don't tell them at first or they won't show up.

YOU WHAT ME TO WHAT!?

YUCK!

I WANTED TO RIDE IT!

Let's cut that baby up!

SPECIAL NOTE: If this metaphor doesn't make you think about being a vegetarian, I don't know what will.

Seeing Into Tomorrow

If history has a lesson to teach us it is that most human beings are lousy guessers. When it comes to being prophetic the majority of us aren't. Still, throughout history a few people seem to have a much better ability than most to see into tomorrow. We call them prophets, visionaries, heretics, or innovators and they see where we're all headed a little clearer.

In life, as well as in business, these better guessers typically have a better chance at survival and seizing opportunities than their less competent compatriots do (other than the heretics who are usually dead). There are always those few who get out of the market before it collapses, leave the town before the tanks arrive, and present the idea right when it's exactly needed. I believe all this has to do with the envisioning of possibilities.

Most people predict tomorrow as a simple extension of today. This step is like the next, today is just like tomorrow, and what was and is will then be. But the visionaries among us are time travelers, they project themselves into the future and see what it really is and could be. There are fewer still who build a road back to the present, empowering themselves and others into activities that make the future their way, the way that they want it to be. This is more than envisioning possibilities, this is the *Envisioning Strategy*.

Envisioning Strategy is best done with the help of quickly-drawn images using the following few steps.

the future tends to be colored by the need in supporting today's choices. If you want to be one of these visionaries, project yourself almost physically into interacting with the future. When there, walk around looking as objectively as possible at what you see, quickly recording those observations.

2 **Generate Possibilities** While looking at the future, stay there and test things out, try your hand at predicting the consequences from various scenarios or possibilities. Then while interacting in this future world, work things out in some detail. Work toward creating a desirable and workable future state or situation. Flesh it out with descriptive details and visually record those details. *Images, or words that create images, offer the best device to remember, refine, and show others what you've seen.*

3 **Plan Steps** Here is where it gets a little tricky. This step is where the dream-like images and the assumed tomorrows are pounded into some kind of reality. It involves thinking and visualizing the dynamics of implementation.

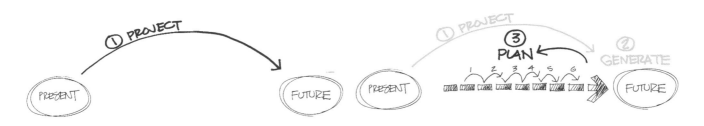

1 **Project Tomorrow** Behind the patterns of choices affecting a person or an organization's behavior is their strategy for handling tomorrow. Most people's strategy is to carry the enormous load of validating today's choices even when trying to take a peak into tomorrow. Anything seen while trying to look at

It is one thing to see tomorrow. It is quite another thing to make tomorrow real. Only a strategy of visualized specific steps will do that. A vision of the future will fade unless a clear picture of what is needed to reach that vision is also created.

4 **Implement Plan** The first thing in implementing the plan is to build a unified vision. Any vision of tomorrow must be effectively shared with others in order to make it a reality. You will need to focus everyone's attention on the future while building consensus, understanding, and support for the implementation of the proposed plan.

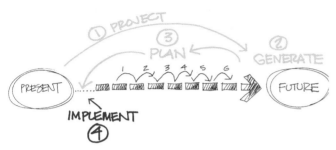

This is where rapid visualization really becomes effective. Participatory images, spontaneous and involving, communicate a future objective without the feeling of being forced on from the higher-ups. By creating images of the future together, people more easily shift thinking and focus their collective involvement in achieving a shared vision.

5 **Measure Progress** When something is measured, something is always achieved. In this step, find a visual way to measure how everyone is doing and where they are as they proceed in creating this future possibility. Nothing works better at this step than using some kind of map and progressively plotting people's progress.

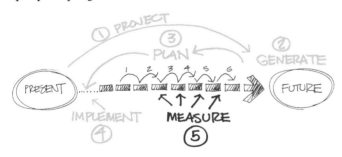

6 **Future Attainment** This is the point to the entire Envisioning Strategy process. Strategy in and of itself has little value. I've been involved on projects where everyone's time and work is eaten up in only working on strategy. If these kind of strategy-only activities don't achieve results they're only mental gymnastics. Any strategy is only as good as the results it achieves.

7 **Review and Adjust** Learn from what you did wrong and right. The best strategic planners and visionaries spend a good deal of time learning from their mistakes. It always surprises me that in so many projects I've been involved with how much this obvious fact is ignored. People, and many of these people should know better, don't take the time to re-

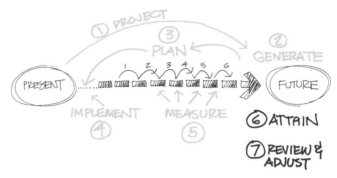

ally study what happened when they tried to make a predetermined future into something real. You would think with the tremendous effort and money invested that some of the resources should be invested in evaluating and refining the entire process.

Summary

As time marches on the future always becomes today. Obviously, sooner or later the future is here. But by using Envisioning Strategy you have more control over what that future will be like when it arrives. Making the entire process with all its steps visual is a tool to better the odds on what kind of tomorrow turns into today.

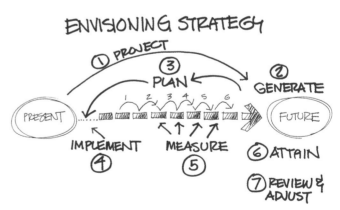

Visualizing Order From Overload

If I hear that we live in the information age one more time I think I'll gag. What else is new? What we need isn't one more person profoundly proclaiming this problem, but what on earth we can do about it. The solutions I've seen presented to give order to our expanding glut of information only seem to pile on more of this growing glut. That's like tossing wood on a fire in order to put it out.

I've found that the only thing that actually helps give some much needed fresh air, as we drown in one more drenching after another of information, are schematic images. These are images that provide structure, meaning, and accessibility to information. A schematic is a diagram, map, or chart that provides a structure to hang information on. These images are like a Christmas tree that provides structure to display all the lights and other decorations. Before the holiday season, the paraphernalia is stuffed into a box in a tangled mass of disorder. The framework of the tree shapes this material into an ordered promotion of meaning and shows the emotional connection. Schematic images also give a meaningful framework to the tangled masses of information.

↓ This diagram was the only way that a complicated subject could be clearly communicated and understood.

Order Fulfillment

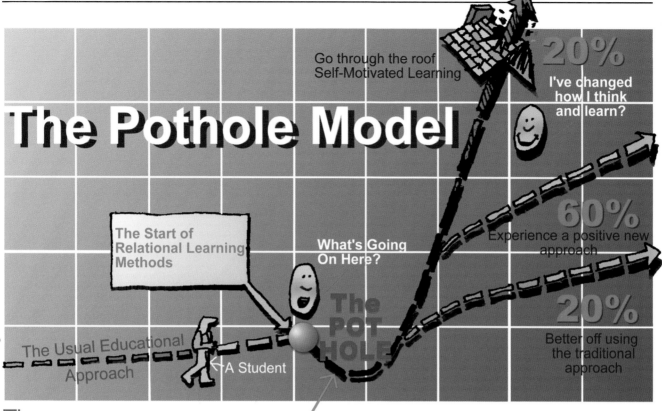

The Pothole Model

Go through the roof
Self-Motivated Learning

20%
I've changed
how I think
and learn?

The Start of
Relational Learning
Methods

What's Going
On Here?

60%
Experience a positive new
approach

The Usual Educational
Approach

A Student

The
POT
HOLE

20%
Better off using
the traditional
approach

Ability →

Time →

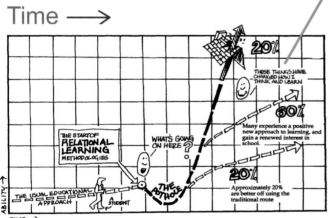

↑ *This chart was the best way I could communicate some unique characteristics of a learning process I implemented with college students.*

← *This is my original sketch.*

↙ *A diagram of a proposed steamship renovation and floating museum.*

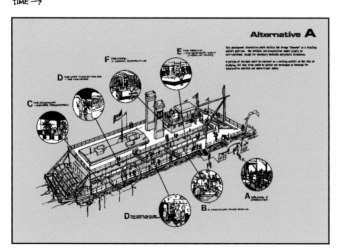

Schematic images are where rapid visualizations really can work miracles in the understanding and communicating of information. I've lost count of the meetings, presentations, conferences, reports, proposals, and sessions where by visually structuring information, clarity and understanding is formed from the chaotic downpour of facts, figures, dates, and data. It amazes me how just a simple chart or graph can so powerfully focus and shift thinking in the human mind.

These schematic images have all sorts of important sounding names such as: critical path schedules, →

NOTE: Both color schematics are just a series of pencil colored sketches done on tracing paper that were scanned into computer image formats, enhanced and then placed over a graduated toned background.

DIAGRAMS

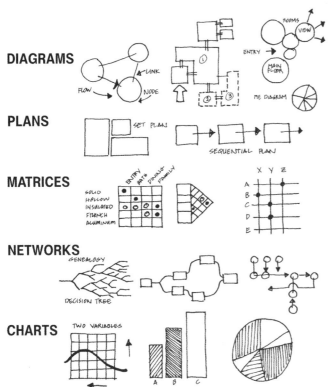

PLANS

MATRICES

NETWORKS

CHARTS

networks, bubble diagrams, matrices, pie charts, Gantt charts, Venn diagrams, PERT charts, maps, and decision trees.

But all of these types of schematics can be summarized into a few crucial elements to be considered when creating an information-organizing image. The following fundamental elements are common to most of these visuals with the important names: hierarchy, process, alternatives, identifiers, size, intensity, timing, and flow.

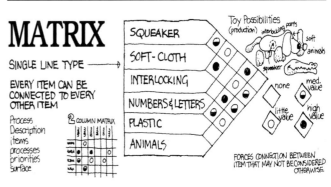

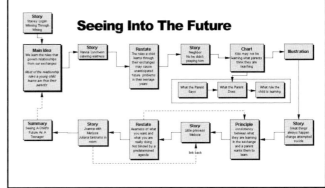

Steps for Visualization

Visualization comes naturally for many of us. But the effort can be enhanced, by anyone, by following these steps:

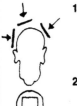

1. **Reduce outside interference.** Find a place where you can be quiet and relaxed. Eliminate outside noise and concentrate on your internal processes. Close your eyes and look through your inner eye.

2. **Create a screen.** As you get images, project them on a movie screen in your mind. You can watch them almost as if you were an outsider.

3. **Evolve the image.** Move from the part you see initially to the whole there is to see, or from the whole to the part. Fill in the details. But don't force it—let the process flow naturally.

4. **Project the image into its context.** If you're working on a book, see your idea in the hands of the reader, and watch his reaction. If you're working on some kind of a device, mentally give it to a user, and watch what he does with it. If you're working on a technique, give it to someone who will apply it, and see how well it works. Mentally put the idea into its context, and test it out.

5. **Transfer the image.** This is the hardest step. Transfer what's in your head into reality. Show others the image. Create your internal view in an external form.

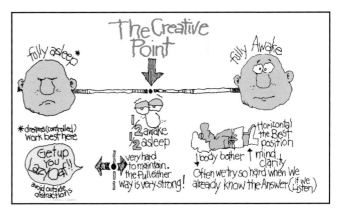

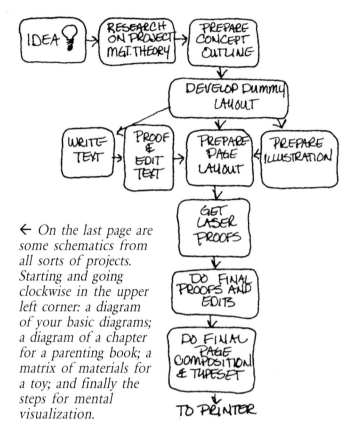

← *On the last page are some schematics from all sorts of projects. Starting and going clockwise in the upper left corner: a diagram of your basic diagrams; a diagram of a chapter for a parenting book; a matrix of materials for a toy; and finally the steps for mental visualization.*

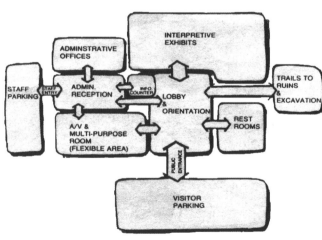

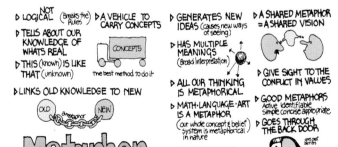

Hierarchy—level of importance

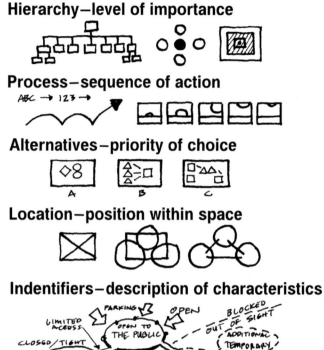

Process—sequence of action

Alternatives—priority of choice

Location—position within space

Indentifiers—description of characteristics

Size—comparison in volume

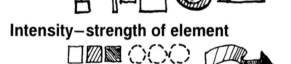

Intensity—strength of element

Timing—relationship with time

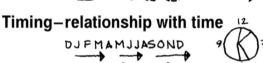
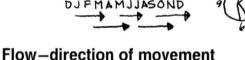

Flow—direction of movement

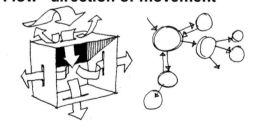

Examples of schematics, starting and going clockwise from the upper left corner: steps involved in producing a brochure; a chart of the basic elements of schematics; a list on how to use a metaphor; and a interrelationship schematic for a visitor center.

Providing a Look Into Tomorrow

There is always the need to show somebody what something proposed for the future will look like. Nothing moves on many projects until key people see how the project will look when it's completed. There is no investment money, no excitement, and no understanding until these individuals have some images placed in front of them.

Drawings of the concepts in some visual form are often the only way to get these key people really involved on a project, with everyone working together

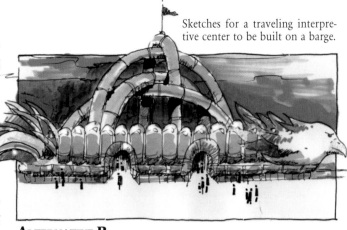

Sketches for a traveling interpretive center to be built on a barge.

ALTERNATIVE B

THEATRE

EXHIBIT AREA

ALTERNATIVE A–DOCKSIDE

GIFT SHOP

BIRD'S EYE–EXPANDED ENTRY

DINNER SHOW

and seeing the same vision. These types of drawings typically take a good deal of time to complete. They are often hard to get the way you want them to look and they are always very expensive. When finished they look like beautiful paintings of idyllic settings and cost as much as a new car.

But I've always had the belief that if you want any more than what I do, go to a good architectural renderer or a professional illustrator. They do a great job, but it's not what I do. In the time it takes these people to do one drawing, You can do a whole collection →

Part of a series of quckly-drawn images for a future theme park.

NOTE: All these drawings were first drawn small with a fine black pen, then colored in pencil, and finally enhanced on the computer, all in a short time (5-8 hrs). It took far more frustating time to collect the information and approval I needed to complete these images than it ever took to actually draw them.

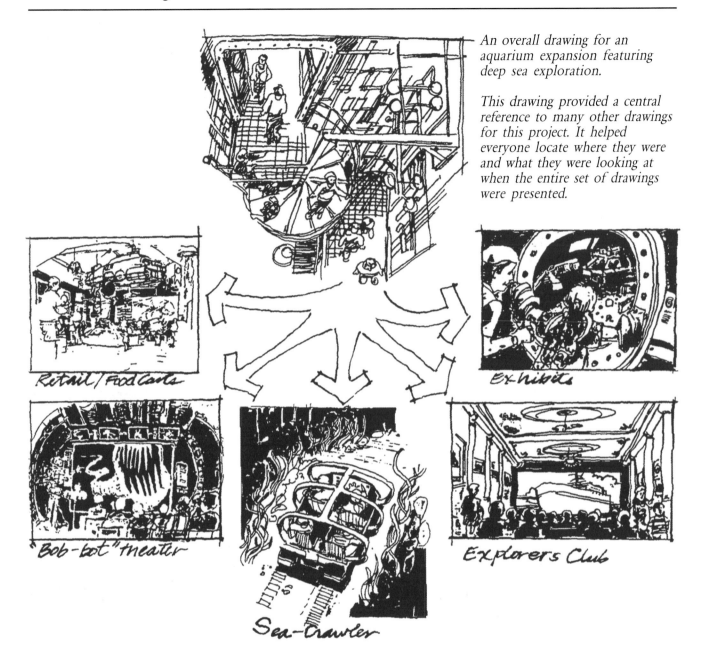

An overall drawing for an aquarium expansion featuring deep sea exploration.

This drawing provided a central reference to many other drawings for this project. It helped everyone locate where they were and what they were looking at when the entire set of drawings were presented.

Retail / Food Carts

Exhibits

"Bob-bot" Theater

Sea-Crawler

Explorers Club

of drawings, each one showing a different view or another part of the project. So I work on creating a large number of drawings, with each one illustrating what an important aspect of the entire future project will look and feel like.

It's like showing someone an entire set of snapshots from the future. I've found that this provides the viewer with a more complete impression than just one drawing could ever do. Many times I've had one painting on one wall stacked up against my visuals filling up the entire other wall.

Guess where all the people in the room go to stand, view, and get a feel or sense of ownership for their project?

These kinds of drawings are concept drawings, providing views of the future with all its interesting possibilities, showing people things, experiences, and interactions they can be deeply involved in on the other side of tomorrow. Drawings illustrating how an idea will work refine the design, evolve alternatives, and build consensus help move a project rapidly toward completion.→

NOTE: This pages drawings were originally done on 8 1/2 X 11 inch sized heavy tracing or 100% cotton bond paper.

*A collection of future envisionings
from a multitude of world-wide
projects: from Africa to Japan to
the Bahamas.*

*Each drawing was unique to each
project, but the rapid visualization
process used to create them was
exactly the same.*

NOTE: Doing these types of drawings first rough on tracing paper,
then faxing them to everyone involved for their input saves time and
increases acceptance later on in the development process.

This page shows examples of Future Visioning. Starting from above, they are: a theme park ride; a miniature golf course; a visitor center; a water park ride; and finally some character development sketches. The techniques I used on all of them are the same.

I've had drawing experts tell me that the above drawings couldn't be done rapidly and that it would take them over 20 or more hours to do any one of them, but remember one thing, they are only a few inches high. The detail and refinement people read into these drawings is an optical illusion.

NOTE: Though drawn fast and small on 8 1/2 X 11 sized paper. The drawings above were enlarged in a wide format printer to 3 feet wide for a presentation. The illusion of detail holds, even when enlarged.

EXHIBIT TREES AND PEOPLE

GIFT SHOP

WELCOME MEET MR. MORTON

THE GREENHOUSE

EXHIBIT TREES IN THE COMMUNITY

EXHIBIT TREES—UP CLOSE AND PERSONAL

I find working on these drawings fun. It is exciting to see what the future will look like as it unfolds and transforms right in front of my eyes on the drawing pad. It's also surprising to me how often these quick visualizations match up to the real thing.

↑ *The above drawings are for a proposed small educational center. Each drawing shows what the visitor would see and experience at important junctions along the tour path.*

There is a synergy that occurs when an intent is visualized. The interaction between a myriad of elements, conditions, and constraints form themselves into something real at the junction point of a simple evolving image. At that point, drawing becomes a living process striving to create more life.

Drawing can be more than something you do in the off-hours from living you life. With me, it has been an essential language that I've had to speak all of my life. I have dyslexia so there is always a mixing of words and ideas inside this thick head of mine. The only thing I've ever found to compensate for that was drawing. Images make sense and order from all that disorder of words and ideas. Since grade school until the present day, drawing is the only language that I'm really comfortable with.

Back in school, teachers would always find my drawings. They would always think it was only my crazy artwork. But it was much more than that. One day a teacher's ruler whacked across my hand to get me to stop drawing and put those silly art pages away. From then on I hid my drawings and how I used visualization from everyone. No one ever knew what I was really doing, that is until this book. Now my visualization secrets are plastered all over its pages.

I also remember being called into a meeting with a school counselor with my what's-he-good-for test scores laying out on his desk in front of him. He motioned for me to sit down. He started to talk a number of times, but withdrew only to attempt to say something again. He seemed at a total loss on what to say to me. Finally he hesitatingly said, "We don't know where to put you. With all the other kids that get tested, it's obvious. But with your test scores we really don't know what to say to you, what to tell you what you could become." Holding up a graph of my scores, he said, "I've never seen anything like this."

The graph looked exactly like an upside down wide-headed nail, the spike at the top being my visual abilities and the head at the bottom being everything else. "Your grades are better than this profile indicates and the only profession we can come up with that in any way fits you is becoming an industrial designer," he added.

When I asked him what an industrial designer was, he said, "It's a guy who designs factories." Not even close, but prophetic anyway. It's what I actually became. But it's about the graph I would like to talk about, and what I've thought a lot about since that day.

The counselor couldn't understand how one part of my score, the visual, could be so high, and why everything else was so low. It actually makes total sense to me now. I was just using my visual abilities to give meaning and order to everything else. You may also have a similar visual bias in some way, maybe not as severe as mine, but it's there. You wouldn't have gotten this far in the book if you didn't. So I would like to end with this one idea.

In this book, drawing is not driven by the usual need to make pretty pictures, but by the need to make sense out of all the information, experiences, and knowledge life throws at us. And when drawing becomes Rapid Visualization, it generates a powerful kind of synergy between how and what we know, how and what we perceive, and our abilities to affect change in both others and ourselves. In other words, take care using these Rapid Visualization tools. They will change you.

About The Author

The glasses are put on or taken off and the mustache grown or shaved depending on sunspot activity.

Kurt is currently a change consultant involved in the concept development, and implementation of organizational and business training. He is also a concept designer, involved in the creation of a worldwide collection of museums, theme parks, and visitors' centers. He has been a professor, a carpenter, an art director, worked on both ends of a cow, and a father (now with too many grandkids to count). He has also been a research and product development director, a president of his own information design business, and calls himself "A reluctant writer," having written over 20 books on a wide variety of subjects.

Kurt has worked for organizations such as The National Arbor Day Foundation, US Air Force, US Army, MGM, LucasArts, Bureau of Land Management, Sun International, The Franklin Institute, The National Park Service, and so on. . . .

"The creative core of all my work," Kurt says, *"centers on the subject matter of this book."* The rapid visualization of ideas and information drives everything he has done. Now after a good deal of friendly arm twisting, he has finally put all his unique visualizing methods into a single book so the rest of us can see how he does it.